Praise for
Landed: The guide to buying property in Japan

"*Landed* is an essential reference for anyone buying real estate in Japan. It is unbiased and full of practical, up-to-date information. Even Japanese buyers can learn a lot from this book."
Nobuo Takenaka
President and CEO
Misawa Homes Co., Ltd.

"Dillon's book is so good that while reading it, I felt like I was an adult in a toy store: Envious of the stuff kids have now that I would have loved to have as a kid. If only I had the information in this book when I was building my house in the 1990s, I wouldn't have ended up with the financial albatross I have now! *Landed* is an essential resource for anyone considering buying the most expensive consumer good in one of the most expensive (and tricky) housing markets in the world. It's even a good read!"
Arudou Debito
Author of *Handbook for Newcomers, Migrants and Immigrants to Japan*, and coordinator of Debito.org

"*Landed* provides valuable and comprehensive information for foreigners interested in purchasing property in Japan. Detailed information, statistics, sample budgets and personal stories make this guide readable and helpful."
Jared Braiterman, Ph.D.
Founder, Tokyo Green Space
tokyogreenspace.com

Landed
The guide to buying property in Japan

Christopher Dillon

DILLON
COMMUNICATIONS
www.dilloncommunications.com

For James and Patricia Dillon

ISBN: 978-988-17147-3-2

The author and publisher have made every effort to ensure the accuracy and completeness of the information in this book but assume no responsibility for errors, inaccuracies or omissions.

This book is published as a general reference and is not intended to be a substitute for professional legal, investment or tax advice. Readers should always obtain independent, professional advice before signing any legal document.

All dollar figures in this book are expressed in United States dollars unless otherwise indicated.

CONTENTS

ACKNOWLEDGEMENTS

I had a lot of help in researching and writing this book.

For generously sharing their time and expertise, I would like to thank Jake Adelstein, Paul Allen, Julian Bailey, Tony Collins, Hank Daaboul, Matt Dening, Mark Dytham, Jason Foutch, Mitsuo Hashimoto, Richard Henderson, Steven Herman, Jun Honma, Koichi Hori, Reiko Kawabata, John Kirch, Simon Klassen, Astrid Klein, Hajime Kojima, David Markle, Erik Oskamp, Toshio Ota, Noriko Oyama, Paul Previtera, Jean-Guy Rioux, Jr., Johan Sekora, Dale Willetts, Steven Windholz and Masaru Yokomizo.

For production assistance, thanks to Mark Darbyshire, Michael Evans, Janice Henderson, Sainbor Kharbithai, Jack Jackson, Nancy Lee, Rickie Lo, Jeff Loucks, Midori Takano and Carey Vail.

Finally, thank you to the creators of the free and open source software—including OpenOffice, Firefox and Zotero—that I used to write and research this book.

INTRODUCTION

Landed: The guide to buying property in Japan was written for anyone purchasing, or thinking of purchasing, a residential, recreational or investment property.

Landed focuses on practical information. It explains the buying process, how to avoid common problems and where to find more information. It doesn't include statistics, economic analysis or cultural information, except as it relates to buying real estate.

In writing *Landed*, I have omitted the sales pitch. I assume that—whether for family reasons, the economic opportunity or the quality of the snow—you want to buy real estate in Japan.

Information asymmetry

For most people, buying real estate is a textbook case of information asymmetry. You might buy one or two properties in your lifetime. When you do, you will use an agent with intimate knowledge of the local market. You will work with a lender who knows the mortgage market inside out. And you will buy from a vendor who is aware of her property's shortcomings, including the upstairs neighbor who likes to entertain until the early hours of the morning. In short, everyone in the process knows more than you do. That puts you at a big disadvantage, especially if you are operating in a second language and with laws and customs that are different from those at home. *Landed* addresses these issues.

This book is also intended to help couples in which one partner is fluent in Japanese and the other is not. Often, this leaves one partner uninformed and places an unfair burden of translation and interpretation on the other, whose property and financial knowledge may not match his language skills.

Inside Landed

Landed: The guide to buying property in Japan opens with "People," which is a brief look at the demographic trends that are shaping Japanese society.

"Your new home" examines the process of buying a new or used condominium or house. It includes information about where and what to buy, the things that make Japan's property market unique and the risks that accompany a real estate purchase.

"Finance" explains how and where to obtain a mortgage, Japan's earthquake insurance system and the tax implications of buying, holding, renting and selling property.

"Special cases" explores the process of working with an architect to custom-design a home. It examines the opportunities available to small investors, explains how to buy a foreclosed home and looks at recreational property in Niseko. It also describes some less conventional investments.

The last section, "Resources," features information to help you manage everything from antiquities uncovered during the building process to utility companies. Notes are included for readers who want to learn more about the topics covered in *Landed*.

A final note

Many things—from immigration policies to lending practices— change quickly, so ensure you have current information before making an important decision. Other elements, such as tax laws, are subject to interpretation or handled on a case-by-case basis. Get expert advice before signing a contract.

Inclusion of a company or organization in *Landed* should not be taken as a recommendation. And if I have omitted a company, it does not mean you should avoid them.

Throughout the book, I use the word "home" to refer to residential dwellings, including condominiums and detached houses. Finally, to avoid "he or she" and "s/he," I alternate between male and female pronouns.

I hope you find *Landed: The guide to buying property in Japan* helpful and look forward to including your comments and suggestions in the next edition of the book.

PEOPLE

DEMOGRAPHIC TRENDS

Japan's population is aging and shrinking. Young people are moving from rural areas and small towns to Tokyo, Osaka and Nagoya, while households are becoming smaller. Each of these trends has long-term implications for the nation's property market and for your investment in Japanese real estate.

Aging

Japan is demographically unique. In no other country do the elderly comprise such a large proportion of the population. From an aging society, with 7% of its population over 65 in 1970, Japan became an aged society (14% over 65) in 1994 and a super-aged society (20% over 65) in 2005. That same year, seniors made up just 12% of the U.S. and 5% of the Indian populations.[1]

The surge in Japan's elderly population has not peaked. Baby boomers, known as *dankaisedai*, will begin turning 65 in 2012. By 2055, more than 40% of the population will be over 65. One person in four will be over 75 by 2025.[2] The Japanese people's longevity is fueling this trend. Girls born in 2007 are expected to live to 86—the world's longest life span—while boys born in 2007 should live 79 years, second only to San Marino.

Many *dankaisedai* benefited from the lifetime-employment system, which is now increasingly rare. Today, "freeters"* and temporary workers comprise a growing proportion of the workforce. These workers receive lower salaries and fewer benefits than permanent, full-time employees and their positions were among the first to be eliminated during the recession that began in 2008. Without a secure job and benefits, young people are less likely to get married, start a family or buy a home, all of which is bad news for Japan's housing market.

Freeters are young people who lack full-time employment.

Unlike Japan's youth, its senior citizens are wealthy. In 2007, 903,000 households had net financial assets of ¥100 million or more and households headed by people over age 60 have more than half of Japan's savings and net worth.[3] Real estate makes up a large proportion of these assets: More than 89% of seniors own their homes,[4] which are mainly freestanding houses.[5] However, this wealth is illiquid. The market for used homes is small and reverse mortgages, which allow seniors to unlock the value of their homes, are not widely available.

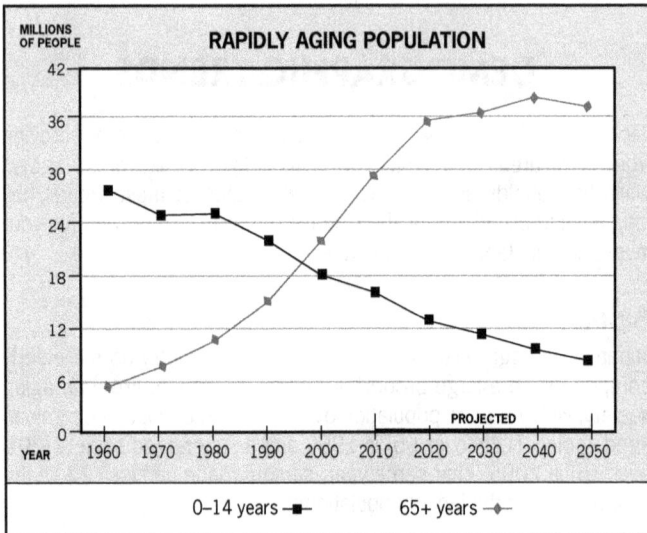

MILLIONS OF PEOPLE

RAPIDLY AGING POPULATION

YEAR

PROJECTED

0–14 years ■   65+ years ◆

Young people will inherit this wealth, but they will have to be patient. In 1970, the eldest child was typically aged 41–45 when his father died and 51–55 when his mother died, which is when children inherit the bulk of their parents' estate. In 2004, the eldest child was about 66 when his mother died. This is significant because the incidence of home ownership increases with age and, by the time people reach their 50s, about 86% are homeowners, further increasing the likelihood that children will not live in the real estate they inherit.

A trend toward smaller families is concentrating Japan's wealth. A person born in 1947, for example, will inherit 20%–25% of her parents' assets. Someone born in 1957 will inherit about half, while a child born in 2005 will receive virtually all of her parents' estate. Again, this increases the likelihood that inherited property will be surplus and sold or rented out. It is also dividing Japan's elderly into two groups: the wealthy, who can afford a comfortable retirement, and those who depend on state assistance to survive. Single-person households, especially women, comprise the bulk of the latter category.

Reconfiguring households

The composition of Japanese households is changing. Japan's population peaked at 127.8 million in 2004,[6] but the number of households will continue to grow until 2015, when over half of the 50.5 million households will comprise singles or married couples living without children. As the number of private households grew, their average size shrank from 3.28 people in 1975 to 2.55 in 2005. This figure is projected to fall to 2.37 in 2025.

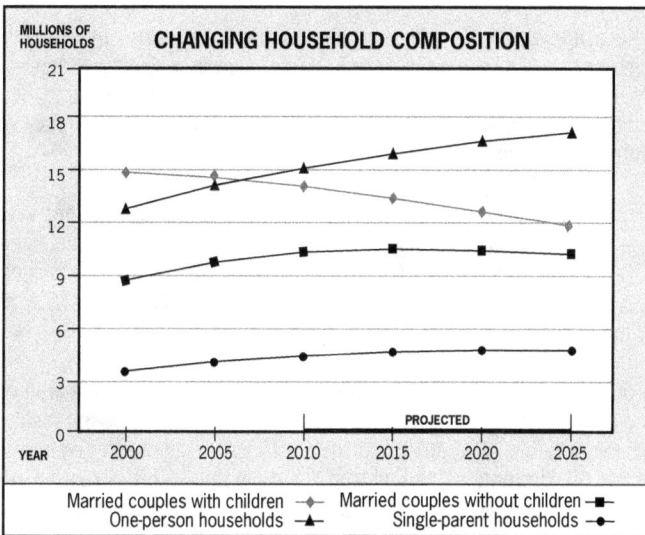

CHANGING HOUSEHOLD COMPOSITION

MILLIONS OF HOUSEHOLDS

Married couples with children — Married couples without children —
One-person households — Single-parent households —

Higher divorce rates are contributing to the growth in households and demand for smaller dwellings. Divorces doubled from 141,689 in 1980 to an all-time high of 289,836 in 2002 before falling to 257,475 in 2006. There has also been an increase in the number of households headed by single mothers, which topped one million for the first time in December 2008. More seniors are divorcing: In 1980, 0.08% of the female and 0.26% of the male population over 60 were divorced. By 2006, these numbers had grown to 0.29% and 0.65%, respectively.

Parents and children living separately are also contributing to the surge in the number of households. Traditionally, aging parents are cared for by their eldest son and his wife. In 1983, about 45% of the elderly population lived this way. By 2003, the proportion had fallen to 15%.

The introduction of the long-term care insurance system (LCIS) in April 2000 made it easier for elderly people to live on their own. The government-run LCIS covers everyone over 65 and individuals between 40 and 65 who have medical conditions that require long-term care. LCIS services range from home visits by healthcare workers to daycare centers and residential facilities for people who need full-time care.

"Parasite singles" are another defining feature of Japan's demography. The phrase, which was coined in 1997 by Professor Masahiro Yamada of Tokyo Gakugei University, describes unmarried people who live with their parents, either by choice or circumstance, often into middle age.

This phenomenon is also common in Italy and Germany. What sets Japan apart is its prevalence. In 2004, nearly half of people aged 20–34 and more than 10% of those aged 35–44 lived with their parents. Parasite singles aged 20–44 comprised over 10% of Japan's total population.[7]

For parasite singles, living with mom and dad means paying little or no rent, avoiding domestic chores and enjoying home-cooked meals. It also lets the children spend their salaries on discretionary items, such as international travel and luxury goods. This arrangement is not necessarily lopsided. Many parents say they appreciate the company of their adult children and look forward to being cared for into their old age.

Parasite singles depress Japan's housing market. One estimate suggests that if just 10% moved out, they would boost housing demand by a million units. In addition, parasite singles are unlikely to complicate their living arrangements by getting married or having children.

A smaller population

Whether you hold it for a year, a decade or a century, you—or your heirs—will sell your Japanese real estate into a market that is smaller than it is today.

From a peak of 127.8 million in 2004, Japan's population is expected to fall to 90.0 million–102.0 million in 2050 and to 37.7 million–64.1 million in 2100.[8] There have been suggestions that even these grim projections may be optimistic as Japan's birthrate is dropping faster than any other nation's.[9]

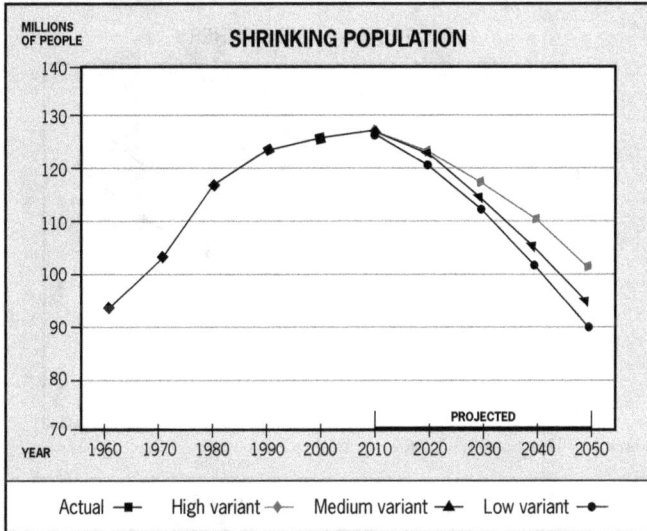

SHRINKING POPULATION

MILLIONS OF PEOPLE

PROJECTED

YEAR   1960   1970   1980   1990   2000   2010   2020   2030   2040   2050

Actual ━■━   High variant ━◆━   Medium variant ━▲━   Low variant ━●━

There are several reasons for the decline. With improved educational and career opportunities, more Japanese women are choosing to remain single. The lifetime nonmarried rate* for women rose from 1.9% in 1960 to 7.3% in 2005. And those who stay single are much less likely to be stigmatized for their decision than women a generation earlier. In 2004, about 40% of the women aged 30–34 in Tokyo were unmarried.

Women who marry are doing so later, at an average age of 28.5 in 2008 versus 24.2 in 1970. Contraceptive pills, which were legalized in 1999, and accessible, socially acceptable abortions give women greater control over when they have children.[10] Consequently, they are choosing to have their first child later, at an average age of 29.5 in 2008 versus 25.6 in 1970. This increases the likelihood that a woman's first child will also be her last.

Pregnancy often spells the end of a woman's career and Japan's work culture is not family-friendly. In fiscal 2008, ended March 31, 2009, only 1.23% of eligible men took child care leave, significantly less than the government's target of 10%.

*The lifetime nonmarried rate is the mean value of the proportion remaining single at ages 45–49 and the proportion remaining single at ages 50–54.

Childbirth costs about ¥500,000 and is not covered by national health insurance, although about 70% of this amount is refunded as an allowance. Despite more than ¥245 billion in child-care-related spending in the fiscal 2009 budget,[11] an estimated 18,000–40,000 children are waiting for places in daycare centers.[12]

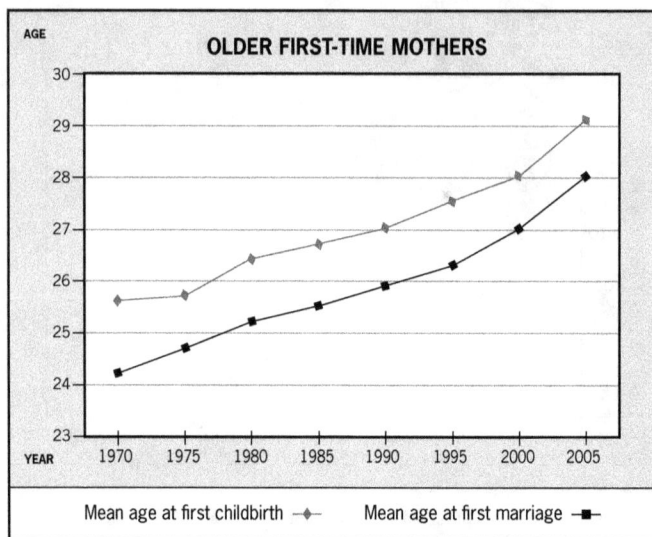

OLDER FIRST-TIME MOTHERS

Mean age at first childbirth ◆   Mean age at first marriage ■

The declining population became a public issue in 1990 after the "1.57 shock," when the total fertility rate for the previous year reached a record low 1.57 children per woman. After nearly two decades, Japan's population-building programs have accomplished little. At 1.21, Japan's estimated 2009 fertility rate ranked 218th out of 224 countries and territories.[13] While this was far below the global replacement rate of 2.33, Japan did place ahead of neighbors South Korea, Taiwan, Singapore and Hong Kong. Home buyers in Japan can also take comfort in the knowledge that this is a world-wide trend. Between 2020 and 2050, the global fertility rate is expected to fall below 2.33.

Immigration

Immigration would seem to be an obvious solution to Japan's shrinking population, but Japan accepts relatively few immigrants. At the end of 2007, there were 2.15 million registered foreign nationals in Japan (up from 1.42 million in 1996), representing 1.69% of the total population, and an estimated 110,000 illegal immigrants. Over 439,000 foreigners had permanent resident status and some 430,000 individuals—mainly people of Korean and Taiwanese descent who were either born in Japan or moved there during Japan's colonial era—were special permanent residents.

The Koreans and Taiwanese are classed as special permanent residents because Japan operates on the principle of *jus sanguinis* (citizenship by descent) rather than *jus soli*, which grants citizenship based on where a person was born. Dual citizenship is technically prohibited and until the Nationality Act was amended in 1985, a child of a foreign father and Japanese mother was not granted Japanese nationality at birth. According to Arudou Debito,* associate professor at Hokkaido Information University, about 20,000 foreigners become naturalized Japanese citizens each year.[14] With a population 2.4 times larger than Japan's, the United States has more than 24 million legal permanent foreign-born residents. Over 600,000 people become naturalized Americans each year.[15]

There is awareness in the business community that Japan needs foreign workers to care for the elderly, pay taxes and support the national pension plan. Groups such as the Japan Association of Corporate Executives (Keizai Doyukai) have suggested offering healthcare, training and pensions to attract unskilled workers to Japan.[16] In 2009, Prime Minister Hatoyama emphasized the importance of creating "an environment that is friendly to people all around the world so that they voluntarily live in Japan."[17]

In the short term, however, the number of foreigners will probably drop. In the spring of 2009, many large international banks, brokerages and insurers slashed head counts and the Japanese government began paying foreign workers ¥300,000 to leave. By the end of August 2009, an estimated 40,000 Brazilians of Japanese descent had returned to Brazil.

Some people will welcome the foreigners' departure. High-profile politicians, including Tokyo Governor Shintaro Ishihara, have cited foreigners as a source of problems and in a 2008 survey of inn operators, more than one-quarter of respondents said they didn't want foreign guests.[17] Many landlords are also reluctant to rent to foreigners, citing communication difficulties, friction with neighbors, worries about tenants conforming to local regulations and difficulties in finding a guarantor.

Japanese names in this book are shown in Western order (first name followed by last name). Arudou Debito, a naturalized Japanese citizen, has stated a preference for his name to appear in the Japanese order (last name followed by first name).

Concentrating

In 2008, for the 13th consecutive year, migration from rural areas and smaller centers added to the total population of Tokyo, Osaka and Nagoya.[18] Forty-one of 47 prefectures experienced net out-migration during the year, with Hokkaido losing 21,129 people, Aomori 9,266 and Nagasaki 8,799.

Japan's third largest metropolitan area and home to much of the country's automotive industry, Nagoya saw net inward migration of 13,525 people in 2008, while Osaka had a net decrease of 11,143.

The Tokyo Metropolitan Area (which comprises the 23 special wards, 26 cities, five towns and eight villages that make up Tokyo-to, plus neighboring Saitama, Chiba and Kanagawa prefectures) benefits from this trend. With a population of about 35 million, the Tokyo area saw net inward migration of 151,696 people in 2008, some 83,000 of whom moved to Tokyo-to.

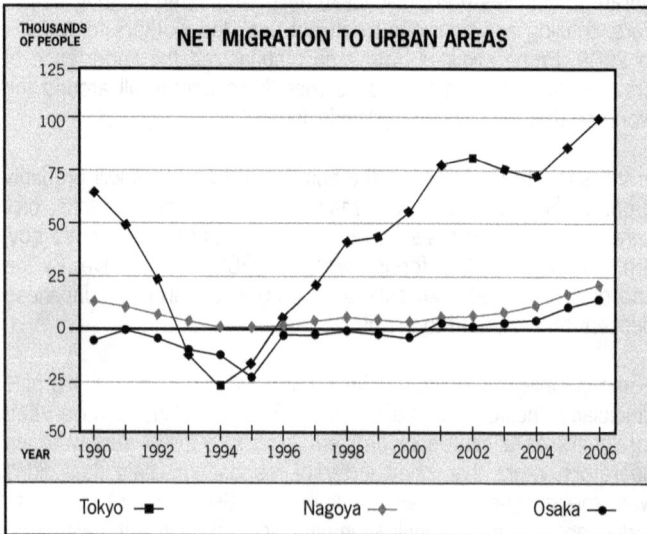

NET MIGRATION TO URBAN AREAS

Tokyo —■—   Nagoya —◆—   Osaka —●—

Japan's largest city, Tokyo is a transport, commercial and cultural hub and home to the national government and many of Japan's leading universities. These businesses and institutions will support long-term demand for homes in central locations and near train and subway stations.

Tokyo is also a magnet for female students and graduates, who are attracted to its cosmopolitan lifestyle and career opportunities. Many of these women are in their prime childbearing years, and when they move to Tokyo their hometowns lose both current and future residents.[19]

Depopulation is a major problem for rural areas. Between 2000 and 2030, mountainous farming areas will lose over one-third of their population, while hilly farming areas will lose more than one-fifth of their people. The average age in rural areas is climbing. In 2000, one person in four in mountainous and hilly farming areas was over 65; by 2030, more than one in three will be a senior. The Ministry of Land, Infrastructure, Transport and Tourism estimates that 400 of the 62,000 communities it classifies as depopulated are in danger of extinction within the next 10 years.[20]

Out-migration is creating real estate bargains in rural areas. But as the population ages and shrinks, and the tax base contracts, it will be difficult for governments and businesses to remain solvent and deliver services. For example:

- In October 2009, the national government ordered 21 municipalities that were in serious financial difficulties to file turnaround plans.

- There is a chronic shortage of doctors, especially obstetricians, in rural areas. Even Tokyo's Aiiku Hospital, where Princess Kiko gave birth to Prince Hisahito in 2006, has trouble recruiting doctors.

- Some 153 gas stations in thinly populated areas in 32 prefectures could be forced to close for lack of business. This is part of a larger trend that has seen the number of stations nationwide drop 4.5% in fiscal 2008 and 30% since fiscal 1994.

- In January 2010, the government announced that 30 rail lines had closed since fiscal 2000. Falling passenger traffic was a key factor behind the closures.

Despite these challenges, rural property can be attractive. But do your homework to ensure you don't get stuck with a property that you cannot sell or enjoy.

YOUR NEW HOME

THE BUYING PROCESS

A logical place to start the buying process is to set a budget, which will help you determine what kind of home you can afford. As a reference point, in early 2008 the average price of a pre-owned detached home in the Tokyo Metropolitan Area˙ was ¥36.5 million. The average condominium was ¥26.4 million.[1]

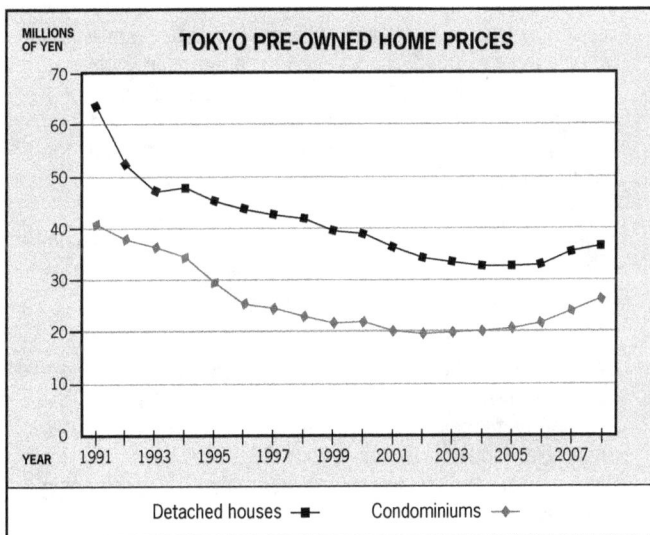

TOKYO PRE-OWNED HOME PRICES

MILLIONS OF YEN

Detached houses ▬■▬   Condominiums ▬◆▬

Then visit one of the Internet listing sites to see what is available at that price. With different combinations of building age, floor space, neighborhood, distance from the nearest train station and commuting time, you should locate a few homes that meet your requirements and preferences. Find two or three examples to eliminate outliers, such as condominiums that have been deeply discounted because of a recent death.

˙The Tokyo Metropolitan Area comprises Tokyo-to and Saitama, Chiba and Kanagawa prefectures.

When you find a property that fits your needs and budget, add 7%–8% to the asking price for closing costs. These include taxes and registration fees, brokerage charges, mortgage origination and appraisal fees, insurance and moving costs. You may want to add 1%–2% for new furniture, appliances or decorations and unexpected delays and other contingencies. If you are buying a condominium, include the monthly condominium management (*kanri-hi*) and building repair (*shuzen tsumitate kin*) fees as well as land rental, parking, rooftop usage, cable TV and Internet fees, if applicable, in your monthly budget. You may also need to pay monthly or annual dues to the local neighborhood association. For sample budgets, see "Choosing a location" and "Investment property."

Price information

Japan's real estate markets are notoriously opaque. This lack of transparency means that, on average, buyers incur over ¥1 million in search costs when they buy a used condominium.[2]

Transaction prices and valuations from real estate appraisers (who use the cost, income and comparable appraisal methods) are usually kept secret. If you are applying for a mortgage, the lender will have the property appraised. You will pay for the appraisal, but the lender will not share the results with you.

To further confuse matters, transaction prices and appraised values differ from the values used to calculate property taxes. As a result, one piece of land can have four valid prices.[3]

Despite the market's inefficiency, local investors have both money and expertise. There is usually a good reason for a property to sell at a discount. Problem properties can present an opportunity for a knowledgeable buyer, but for the unsuspecting they can be a costly, time-consuming nightmare.

Many buyers rely on magazines such as *Suumo* (www.suumo.jp, Japanese only) for market information. Advertising fliers and real estate agents' window displays are also helpful.

The Ministry of Land, Infrastructure, Transport and Tourism (MLIT) maintains an interactive, bilingual Website that provides historical sales data dating to the third quarter of fiscal 2005 (www.land.mlit.go.jp/webland).

Other information sources include the MLIT's quarterly *Land Price Look Report* and *Monthly Marketing Report on Lands*, which provide broad-brush data on pricing trends. Similar information is available from the Land Institute of Japan (www.lij.jp), the Japan Real Estate Institute (www.reinet.or.jp) and Miki Shoji (www.e-miki.com).

Japan's answer to the Multiple Listing Service in the United States and Canada is called REINS (Real Estate Information Network System). REINS contains a great deal of data, but is only available to licensed real estate firms.

Akasaka Real Estate (www.akasakarealestate.com) maintains a proprietary database covering Tokyo's 23 wards.

When you have an approximate budget, start shopping for a mortgage. Some foreign lenders will let you submit a mortgage application without supporting documents and give you an indicative mortgage amount, interest rate and loan-to-value ratio (the mortgage amount as a percentage of the purchase price). These figures will be based on the lender's policies, market conditions and on your taxable income, outstanding debts, employment history, immigration status and other factors. If you submit a mortgage application with supporting documents, Japanese and foreign lenders will often preapprove your application. At this point, the mortgage amount and interest rates are for your guidance and are not binding on the lender.

Knowledge of the local housing market, sale prices and your ability to borrow will help you decide whether buying a home is a viable option. If it isn't and you would still like exposure to the real estate market, you can buy an investment property, stocks or mutual funds.

Buying a pre-owned home

1. The buyer sets a budget and determines his requirements, including size and location.

2. If financing is required, the buyer researches lending rates and terms and shortlists lenders.

3. The buyer submits a mortgage application to the lender and receives indicative approval. (This is optional and only available from foreign banks.)

4. The buyer submits a mortgage application with supporting personal documents to the lender and receives preapproval (optional).

5. The buyer finds a suitable neighborhood, building or home.

6. The buyer signs a contract appointing the real estate agent to negotiate on his behalf.

7. On the buyer's behalf, the real estate agent negotiates the price, closing date and other terms with the vendor.

8. On the buyer's behalf, the real estate agent makes a purchase offer to the vendor.

9. The vendor accepts the purchase offer.

10. The real estate agent reads the explanation of important matters.

11. The buyer, the vendor and their real estate agents execute a sale and purchase (S&P) agreement. The buyer pays a deposit to the vendor, who issues a receipt. The property is removed from the market until the sale closes or is canceled.

12. The buyer submits a mortgage application (with supporting personal and property documents as well as copies of the S&P agreement and explanation of important matters) to the lender for formal approval.

13. The lender reviews the mortgage application, appraises the home and approves the mortgage. A guarantor is arranged, if needed.

14. If the mortgage is from a Japanese lender, the buyer joins a group life insurance plan.

15. The sale closes. Taxes and other costs are prorated to the closing date. The balance of the purchase price is transferred to the vendor, who surrenders the keys and title. The buyer pays the real estate agent's commission and judicial scrivener's fee, arranges fire insurance and takes possession of the property.

16. The judicial scrivener registers the property in the buyer's name at the Legal Affairs Bureau and pays the registration and license tax on behalf of the buyer.

17. The buyer inspects the property to ensure everything is as recorded in the fixture checklist.

18. The buyer pays the real estate acquisition tax, if applicable.

Shopping for a home

With indicative or preapproval from the lender, you can begin shopping for a home. Return to the Internet listing sites and dig a little deeper: Compare trendy and less-desirable neighborhoods, old and new buildings, prestigious and second-tier builders, and houses and condominiums. These Websites will also help you gauge the premium for living on a prestigious train or subway line, near a train or subway station, or close to the city center.

This information will help you narrow your search to one or two neighborhoods. Wander around the area and consult friends, relatives and coworkers who live nearby. When you are confident that you would like to live in the district, arrange to view prospective homes through the Internet listings or a real estate agent's office at the nearest station. If the agent is finding properties for you, give him a clear written explanation of what you want. This will avoid confusion and make it easier to brief a second agent, if necessary.

When you have found a suitable property, you will sign an agreement appointing the agent to act on your behalf. This represents a significant commitment for the agent, who is unlikely to sign a contract unless he believes you are serious, likely to complete the purchase and able to qualify for financing.

Real estate agents

At the end of fiscal 2006, there were more than 130,000 licensed real estate firms in Japan, most of which were small and medium-sized businesses.

Real estate firms (*takuchi tatemono torihiki gyosha*) focus on specific neighborhoods. Their local knowledge can help you avoid problems like large redevelopment and infrastructure projects. Agents' listings are usually current and agents often know about attractive properties that never appear on the Internet. Homes can remain listed on the Internet until or even after the sale closes, which can make a Web-based search frustrating.

Real estate agents charge a standard sales commission of 3.15%, plus ¥63,000. Discounts can sometimes be negotiated and agents are allowed to work for and receive commissions from both the buyer and vendor.[4] Agents are prohibited from disclosing pricing information they have learned from dealings with a third party.[5]

If you buy a new home (whether completed or off-the-plan) from a developer or from a tied agent, you don't pay a sales commission. But remember that the agent is working for the developer, not you.

Agents are licensed by the government and must renew their license every five years. Licenses use this format: Hyogo (4) 12345. Hyogo is the prefecture where the license was issued, (4) indicates the license has been renewed four times and 12345 is the license number.

Because it is difficult to pass the real estate agents' exam, the person handling your purchase may not be a licensed agent. The company owner may not hold a license, either. But the person who reads the explanation of important matters must be a licensed agent.

Three types of brokerage agreements apply to property sales. In an exclusive agreement, only the appointed agency may sell the property and the vendor cannot sell the property to a buyer that she has found independently. In a semi-exclusive agreement, only the appointed agency may sell the property, but the vendor can sell the property to a buyer she has found. A general agreement lets the vendor sell the property through multiple agencies and to buyers that she has found. Agents like exclusive agreements because they can collect a commission from the buyer and vendor. For this reason, some agents only show properties for which they have an exclusive contract.

Beware what Professor Robert B. Cialdini calls "setup properties" in his book *Influence: The Psychology of Persuasion*.[6] Agents will show you ugly, overpriced homes to set your expectations before showing you nicer, better priced ones. The second group will seem far more appealing after you've seen the first batch, even if the second group isn't particularly attractive.

Duke University Professor Dan Ariely describes another technique for focusing a buyer's attention. The agent shows a customer three desirable, similarly priced homes: two colonial and a contemporary. One of the colonial homes, which Ariely calls the "decoy," needs repairs and is offered at a discount. The decoy serves as a point of comparison and makes the customer more likely to ignore the contemporary and buy the undiscounted colonial home.[7]

The agent will prepare a nonbinding offer (*kaitsuke shomei*, also known as a *fudosan konyu moshikomisho*). If the property is desirable and competitively priced, the agent will include background information about you, such as your health and employment history, how long you have been searching and your ratio of cash to borrowed funds. This information differentiates you from competing bidders and demonstrates that you are a serious buyer who is likely to obtain financing.

If you are shown a desirable, attractively priced property, you may have to buy it immediately. The more you know about property prices, the neighborhood and the market in general, the better prepared you will be to assess the risk in such a decision.

Price is the key negotiating point with pre-owned properties, followed by the size of the deposit (also known as earnest money) and the buyer's ability to arrange financing. If the property has been on the market for some time, a cash offer can make it easier for the agent to negotiate a discount. Because Japanese buyers prefer new homes and fewer new homes are being built, many developers refuse to negotiate on price. However, it may be possible to negotiate other concessions.

Buying from the elderly

Elderly people own much of Japan's residential property. About 80% of elderly people live in freestanding homes, versus about 57% of the total population.[8] Over 89% of the elderly own their homes, with the land under these dwellings representing a large proportion of the households' wealth.[9]

In the United States, the United Kingdom and other countries, as couples age and their children leave, many people sell their house, move into a smaller home and use the sale proceeds to fund their retirement. Retirees often downsize from a detached home to a condominium or a retirement community, where someone else can handle the maintenance and repairs.

Because of Japan's small market for pre-owned homes, elderly people frequently live in houses that no longer meet their needs. These homes are often too big, expensive to heat and cool and difficult to clean and maintain. In addition, many four- and five-story buildings in 1960s-era new towns lack elevators.[10]

Despite these drawbacks, one survey of new town residents found 70% of respondents aged 45 and above wanted to stay in their present homes.[11] The combination of family, friends and familiar surroundings means elderly people may be less motivated to sell than you might expect. Being a patient, pleasant buyer can sometimes make a difference, if the owner is not in a hurry to sell.

The explanation of important matters

After the real estate agent has negotiated the price, closing date and other conditions, he prepares the explanation of important matters (*juyou jikou setsumeisho*). Several days before the sale and purchase agreement (*baibai keiyakusho*) is executed, you should receive a copy of the explanation of important matters. You can retain a local lawyer (*bengoshi*) to review the explanation of important matters for you.

However, it is not unusual to make an offer, negotiate a price and sign a sale and purchase (S&P) agreement for a desirable, attractively priced property in one day. If you have a lawyer review the explanation of important matters, you will probably lose the property to a less cautious buyer.

The explanation of important matters is read aloud by a licensed real estate agent, who is liable for its accuracy, before the S&P agreement is executed. Jason Foutch of Century 21 Smica Create in Tokyo says he has seen this process take as little as 30 minutes and as long as 11 hours. The buyer, vendor and their real estate agents apply their registered seals (*jitsu-in*) to the explanation of important matters and a copy is sent to the lender if the borrower applies for a mortgage.

While the S&P agreement is short and simple, the explanation of important matters is long and complex. It is broadly analogous to the terms and conditions of a sales contract in the West, and outlines the payment schedule, warranty terms, title registration and conditions under which the sale may be canceled.

In preparing the explanation of important matters, the real estate agent researches and completes a 46-item checklist covering a range of issues (see "Risk factors") that could interfere with a buyer's ability to use, enjoy and obtain full value from the property. This includes:

- The presence of buried antiquities in the area.

- Whether the building has been tested for asbestos and the results of these tests.

- The presence of termites in the structure.

- Whether there has been a recent death, suicide, murder, rape or other violent crime on the premises.

- Whether the area has a history of floods, subsidence or landslides.

- The presence of soil contamination, which will cause the contract to be canceled if a new house cannot be safely built on the land.

- Fire, damage or other structural problems affecting the building.

- Leftover items, such as pipes, wells, septic tanks or building foundations, that the buyer would have to remove if he is erecting a new structure.

In the case of asbestos or soil contamination, the legal concept of strict liability may apply. Under strict liability, the current owner is liable for cleaning up a polluted site, even if the owner was not negligent in causing the contamination.[12]

Land, structure and fixture checklists

Before the sale and purchase agreement for a pre-owned home is executed, the vendor completes two checklists. Like the S&P agreement, these forms include spaces for comments and copies are available for the vendor, buyer and their real estate agents. The vendor explains the contents of the checklists to the buyer and the buyer and vendor attach their registered seals to the document.

The Association of Real Estate Agents of Japan (www.homenavi. or.jp/frk) produces four color-coded checklists that are commonly used in the industry.

- **Blue,** for the equipment, fittings and appliances in a pre-owned house.

- **Pink,** for the land and structure of a pre-owned house.

- **Purple,** for the equipment, fittings and appliances in a pre-owned condominium.

- **Orange,** for the structure of a pre-owned condominium.

Fixture checklist

On the blue or purple form, the vendor lists the number and condition of the fixtures, appliances and other items that are included in the sale. When the buyer takes possession of the property, he uses the checklist to ensure nothing has changed since the S&P agreement was executed. These lists cover:

- **Water heater.** Gas-, electric- or solar-powered heaters; boiler.

- **Kitchen.** Sinks, water filter, stove, oven, grill, extractor fan, dishwasher.

- **Bathroom.** Shower stall, bathtub, basin, toilet and accessories, bathwater heater, dehumidifier, mirrors, mirror defogger, washing machine pan, taps, drains.

- **Heating and cooling.** Reverse-cycle air conditioners/heaters; split-type or window-mounted air conditioners; heaters; floor-heating systems; ventilator fans; central heating, ventilating and air-conditioning systems.

- **Electrical.** Indoor and outdoor lighting fixtures and associated switches; circuit breaker panel; electrical outlets; door bell; conventional or video intercom; security system; TV antenna.

- **Storage.** Kitchen cabinets, underfloor storage, shoe cabinet, built-in shelving.

- **Doors and windows.** Interior and exterior doors; screen doors; shutters; Japanese sliding doors (shoji); windows.

- **Other.** Curtains and curtain rods; balcony or deck; garage or carport; garden shed; trees and stones in garden; fences and gates.

Land and structure checklist

On the pink or orange form, the vendor states, to the best of her knowledge, the condition of the building and land. If vacant land is being sold, building-related information may be omitted. If a condominium is being sold, the land-related details may be omitted. See "Risk factors" and "Resources" for additional information on the issues listed below.

Property condition

- **Water leaks.** Previous or current leaks, dates and locations, and remedial actions taken.

- **Termites.** Previous or current infestations, dates and locations, and remedial actions taken.

- **Corrosion.** Locations, remedial actions taken and possible causes.

- **Drainpipes.** Blockage or damage to drainpipes.

- **Inclination.** Parts of the building that are not level and the direction in which they tilt.

- **Reform.** Any renovation work done and the name of the contractor.

- **Fire or other structural damage.** Date, extent and location.

- **Boundary or boundary marker violations.** Location and nature of the violation.

- **Pipes.** Water, drain or gas pipes on the property that are owned by third parties.

- **Subsidence.** Parts of the property where subsidence has been observed and work undertaken to reinforce the building foundations.

- **Residual structures.** Septic tanks, pipes or foundations from a demolished building.

- **Soil contamination.** Pollution affecting the property, including problems caused by previous owners or neighbors.

- **Flooding.** Causes, dates and parts of the property that were affected.

- **Neighborhood building plans.** Construction plans of which the vendor is aware.

- **Noise, vibrations, odors, etc.** Anything that could interfere with the buyer's enjoyment of the property, such as noise from a nearby school, a karaoke lounge or train tracks.

- **Radio frequency interference.** Radio or television channels affected.

- **Neighborhood association.** The name and contact information for the local neighborhood association.

- **Other information.**

Documents

In this section, the vendor states whether she has commissioned any of the work listed below and if she is willing to transfer plans, test results, certificates or related documents to the buyer.

- Architectural drawings for the original building.

- Reform, renovations or repairs.

- Asbestos surveys.

- Seismic evaluations.

- House performance assessments.

- Materials from previous owner.

- Name of agent through which the vendor purchased the property.

- Notes. This includes contact details for vendors, such as propane suppliers, and other information, such as the fact that the company that built the house went bankrupt, for example. This section usually states that the vendor will dispose of any garbage before the buyer takes possession.

The sale and purchase agreement

Most straightforward transactions use a standard S&P agreement, which has variations for vacant land, detached houses and condominiums. These forms are printed by real estate agencies and industry bodies such as the Association of Real Estate Agents of Japan. Detailed contracts are used for large or complex transactions, such as commercial deals.

The sale is legally binding when there is offer and acceptance, which usually occurs on execution of the S&P agreement. In Japan, it is possible to enter a binding oral contract, so buyers and vendors should be careful when negotiating.

Executing the S&P agreement

It is possible to execute an S&P agreement with a signature, but local buyers and vendors use a registered seal. It takes a day to have a seal made at a stamp (*hanko*) shop. The seal is then registered at your local ward office, which issues a card bearing the seal's registration number. The ward office also issues a document (*inkan toroku shomeisho*) that certifies that the seal has been registered.

Buyers usually pay a deposit of 10% of the purchase price or ¥10 million, whichever is less. The deposit is paid in cash or by banker's draft when the S&P agreement is executed. It is sometimes possible to make a smaller deposit or desirable to pay more than 10% if you are bidding on a property that is in demand.

S&P agreements often include a clause stating that the sale is contingent on the buyer obtaining financing. Vendors seeking a quick sale may exclude this clause from the S&P agreement. A buyer's negotiating position is stronger if he knows he can arrange financing or pay cash.

If a translation of the S&P agreement—or any other document used in the transaction—is provided, it should be considered a reference. Only the Japanese document is legally enforceable and few Japanese companies will execute an English-language document.

S&P agreement contents

A typical S&P agreement includes the following information:

- **Land.** The location, lot number, category and size of the land.

- **Building.** The building's location; structural details, including size, construction material, number of floors, size of each floor and type of roof; and any special provisions relating to the land or building. For condominiums, the S&P agreement will include the monthly condominium management and building repair fees, information about the building's long-term maintenance plan and the deed of mutual covenant, which specifies the rights and obligations of the individual condominium owners and the building owners' committee (also known as the union of owners or *kanri kumiai*). It will also indicate whether the building is on leased land and the monthly rent, if applicable.

- **Money.** The total sum payable, showing the amounts for the land, building and consumption tax; the deposit paid when the S&P agreement was executed; and the due date and amount of any partial payments. Consumption tax only applies to the building, not the land, and is only payable if the vendor is a company.

- **Logistics.** The date the property will be delivered to the buyer; the date the buyer will assume responsibility for taxes, utility bills and other expenses; the deadline before which the sale can be canceled by either party with only the forfeit of the deposit; and whether the sale is contingent on the buyer obtaining financing and, if so, the name of the lender, amount of the mortgage and financing deadline.

- **Special provisions.** Any special terms agreed between the vendor and buyer, such as an organized crime exclusion clause (*boryokudan furonto kigyou sono jitsunou to taisaku*), which protects both parties if the yakuza are found to be involved.

- **Description of the transaction.** The names of the vendor and buyer and acknowledgment that they have entered into an S&P agreement for the property described on the date specified.

- **Identification.** The names, addresses and seals of the vendor, buyer and both real estate agents. The agents must provide their registration number and the name of their company president.

- **Stamp tax.** The S&P agreement will have a place to attach the stamps used to pay stamp tax on the transaction.

- **Terms and conditions.**
  - » The property is sold on an as-is basis, unless otherwise agreed.

  - » The buyer will pay the deposit when the S&P agreement is executed.

  - » Both parties waive any claim for compensation if the surveyed size of the property differs from the size indicated on the S&P agreement by less than one square meter (optional).

  - » The property and its title will be transferred to the buyer when the vendor has received full payment.

  - » The vendor will confirm the property's boundaries when the vendor delivers the property to the buyer.

  - » The vendor will transfer the property's title to the buyer free of all liens and encumbrances.

  - » The vendor is responsible for any damage to the property before it is delivered to the buyer.

  - » The buyer will forfeit his deposit if he cancels the sale before the agreed deadline. The vendor will pay the buyer double the amount of his deposit if she cancels the sale before the deadline.

» If either party fails to complete the transaction after the deadline, they will pay the other party a penalty equal to 20% of the purchase price, regardless of the actual damages incurred. If the buyer fails to complete the transaction, the vendor will repay the money received from the buyer less the 20% penalty. If the vendor fails to complete the transaction, the vendor will repay the money received from the buyer plus the 20% penalty.

» If the S&P agreement states that the buyer requires financing to complete the purchase and he is unable to obtain financing, the buyer may cancel the sale up to the date specified on the S&P agreement without paying a penalty. The vendor must return the buyer's deposit, but no interest is payable.

» Issues not addressed above will be handled in accordance with the Japanese Civil Code, other laws and trade practices for the real estate industry. Both parties will try to resolve any disputes through good-faith consultations. If consultations fail, the dispute will be subject to the jurisdiction of the court where the property is located, or another court that is agreed by both parties.

Closing

If you are paying cash and have made the necessary arrangements, the transaction can be completed the same day the S&P agreement is signed. Otherwise, closing will occur when the lender approves your mortgage.

After the mortgage has been approved, the buyer, vendor, their real estate agents and the judicial scrivener (*shiho-shoshi*) meet at the office of the lender or vendor's agent. The fixed property tax and urban planning tax are prorated to the date of the closing, and any other adjustments to the sale price, such as tenants' security deposits, are made.

The buyer completes the registration documents, the buyer and vendor execute the remaining sale documents and the lender transfers the balance of the purchase price to the vendor, sometimes in cash. The vendor surrenders the title deed and keys to the property. The buyer arranges fire insurance, takes possession of the property, reviews the items on the blue or purple checklist and reports any defects or shortfalls to their real estate agent.

The judicial scrivener immediately files an application with the Legal Affairs Bureau (*houmukyoku*) to record the change in ownership, and pays the registration and license tax. The buyer and vendor pay their own costs, such as the judicial scrivener and real estate agent's fees.

Several weeks after the closing, the buyer receives an invoice for the real estate acquisition tax. If the home is new, an inspector from the Tax Department will conduct an appraisal. Depending on the results of the appraisal and the applicable exemptions, this tax may be waived.

Nonresidents buying an investment property are required to file a "Report Concerning Acquisition of Real Property in Japan or Rights Related Thereto," with the Bank of Japan within 20 days of the purchase. Buyers are not required to file the report if the property is used as a residence for the buyer, his relatives or employees; to house a business or nonprofit business; or if the property is purchased from another nonresident.[13]

Title transfer

In Japan, the seller is required to deliver title free and clear of liens and encumbrances. Title transfer is handled by a judicial scrivener, a specialist lawyer who confirms the documents needed for title registration and submits the application to the registry (*tokibo*) at the Legal Affairs Bureau on behalf of the buyer.[14] The judicial scrivener's fee is negotiable and is typically ¥150,000 to ¥180,000. Fees increase if there are joint owners or multiple liens. Judicial scriveners can also register mortgages, as well as land and building leases.

Land and buildings are registered separately. Under the Law of Real Estate Registration (Law No. 123 of 2004), all buildings are required to be registered. However, some buildings remain unregistered until they are sold.

The real estate registry is open for public inspection. Each entry contains the following information: a description of the property; the name of the current owner and date of acquisition; the names of previous owners; injunctions or attachments issued against the property; and encumbrances such as mortgages, easements and leases.[15] Some records are incomplete because of damage sustained in natural disasters and World War II.

In Japan, it is hard to obtain irrefutable proof of good title. An entry in the real estate registry is evidence of registered rights, but it is not absolute proof of those rights. As a result, a buyer must rely on the judicial scrivener and real estate agent's representations and warranties about the quality of the title. There is no state guarantee of title or title-guarantee or escrow companies in Japan, and Japanese banks will not lend unless they have first lien on the property.

Warranty periods

The warranty period depends on the vendor and the nature of the defect. When pre-owned homes are sold, the warranty period can be shortened or lengthened and the S&P agreement and explanation of important matters amended accordingly.

If problems are discovered during the warranty period, they are resolved through a three-step process that starts with the real estate agents mediating the dispute. If the real estate agents are unable to arrive at a satisfactory solution, lawyers are brought in. If the lawyers cannot solve the problem, the two parties find themselves in court.

Pre-owned homes

For the fixtures, equipment and appliances listed on the blue or purple form, the warranty is seven days from the date of the closing. Buyers should check everything thoroughly, including seasonal items such as heaters and air conditioners that may not be used for several months after the closing.

For pre-owned homes and condominiums, the warranty for major structural defects is three months if the vendor is an individual. If the vendor is a company, the warranty period is one year. If the vendor is a licensed real estate company, the warranty period is two years.

The balance of a new home warranty can sometimes be transferred to a second owner.

New homes

Under the Act for Execution of Defect Warranty Liability (AEDWL), the warranty period for major structural defects in new homes is 10 years. The AEDWL requires developers to buy insurance or participate in a deposit program, so that buyers will be covered by a 10-year warranty even if the developer becomes insolvent. For detached houses, the warranty applies to the foundations, walls, columns, roof trusses, sills, diagonal members, floor slabs, roof slabs and horizontal framing members, while roofs, exterior walls and openings for doors and windows are guaranteed against rainwater leakage. For condominiums, the foundations, pilings, walls, and floor and roof slabs are guaranteed, while roofs, exterior walls, openings for doors and windows as well as drainage pipes are guaranteed against leaks. Buyers can extend the warranty to 20 years and include parts other than the basic structural elements.[16]

Other parts of a new home, such as kitchens, bathrooms and individual appliances, are covered by separate warranties. These manufacturers' warranties range in length from a few months to several years. Many builders offer free after-sale maintenance and repair services as a way of enhancing their brand image and maintaining contact with clients.

CHOOSING A LOCATION

If you plan to live in the property you are buying, your needs and preferences, rather than just economic factors, will shape your choice of location. Proximity to railway and subway stations, employment, schools, family, shopping and recreational facilities will influence your decision.

For a given budget, buyers must choose between a smaller, centrally located home and a larger dwelling further from the city center. City living offers convenience and access to more shopping and entertainment choices. Drawbacks include more noise, traffic and air pollution. Large cities also charge higher urban planning taxes.

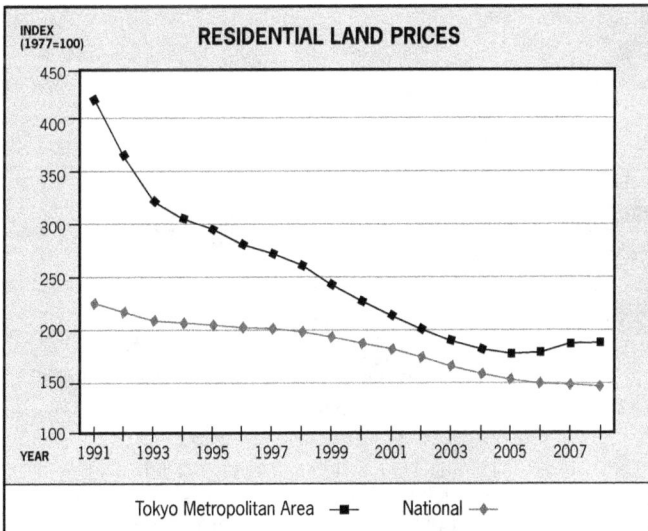

Regardless of the location, southern exposure is popular because it provides more sunlight. This is both an aesthetic benefit and useful for photovoltaic installations, which are increasingly common in Japanese homes. Hilltop dwellings are prestigious and perceived as safer in earthquakes and floods.

Research

Buying or building a home is a major undertaking, so you will want to ensure you like the neighborhood before you sign a sale and purchase agreement. Researching the area and its history on the Internet or at the public library is a good start.

Some people take this a step further by renting an apartment before they buy. Renting can be a good idea if you are moving to an area that is significantly more or less expensive than your old neighborhood. Research by Professor Dan Ariely shows that buyers use the price of their old home as an "anchor" when they buy a new home. This often results in people buying a smaller dwelling when they move into a more expensive area and buying a larger home when they move into a less expensive neighborhood.[1]

At a minimum, walk around the new neighborhood during the day and night, during the week and on weekends. Try the train or subway service between the nearest station and your workplace during rush hour. Investigate services, such as grocery stores, restaurants, hospitals and schools, that you will use.

Bad neighbors

When shopping for a home, avoid:

- Flood zones.

- Reclaimed land, which is at risk of liquefaction during an earthquake.

- Cemeteries and crematoria.

- "Red-light" districts, such as Tokyo's Kabukicho, Fukuoka's Nakasu and Sapporo's Susukino.

- Neighborhoods with a *burakumin* or wartime history. In Tokyo, one such location is the site of the former Sugamo Prison (now Sunshine City) in Ikebukuro, where war criminals were executed after World War II.

- Yakuza offices.

- Flag lots, which are square or rectangular parcels of land that are only accessible by a narrow strip of land. The access path resembles a flagpole.

- Current and former industrial zones. The area around the Port of Tokyo, for example, is home to garbage incinerators as well as treatment facilities for sewage and polychlorinated biphenyls (PCBs). For more information, see "Risk factors."

Kabukicho is one of Tokyo's best-known red-light districts.

Finally, find out whether large infrastructure or urban renewal projects are planned for the area. The noise, dust and traffic disruptions that accompany redevelopment initiatives, such as Tokyo Midtown and Roppongi Hills, can degrade your quality of life over the short term. However, these projects often revitalize fading neighborhoods and drive property prices higher. A redevelopment project is now planned for Tokyo's Shinjuku 3-chome, near the Park Hyatt Hotel.

Transportation

Homes near train or subway stations command higher prices and rents. They also offer better access to shops and restaurants, which cluster around stations. Stations also attract vehicular and pedestrian traffic and the sound trucks used by campaigning politicians and other groups.

Real estate listings include the walking time to the nearest station, which is based on 80 meters per minute of walking time. There are two ways to calculate walking time. The first measures the actual, street-level distance to the nearest station entrance, but ignores time spent waiting at traffic lights. The second measures the distance "as the crow flies" over the tops of buildings and other obstacles. With the second method, a walk that is advertised as 10 minutes can easily take twice as long.

A 2007 paper published by the Center for Spatial Information Science (CSIS) at the University of Tokyo observed that the price of used condominiums in the Tokyo area fell when the walking time to the nearest railway station exceeded 12 minutes. Prices fell again at the 17-minute mark, the point at which most people are believed to take a bus, bicycle or car to the station.

As Japan's population continues to age and a 10-minute walk to the station becomes more onerous, the premium for homes near train and subway stations should increase. The government's "compact city" initiative—which encourages the construction of hospitals, nurseries, government offices and other essential facilities near railway stations—will also support this trend.[2]

The CSIS paper also examined the effect of station-to-station commuting time on condominium prices. The authors noted that prices fell when daytime travel between the station nearest the condominium and seven target stations—Ikebukuro, Shibuya, Shinagawa, Shinjuku, Tokyo and Ueno on the Yamanote Line, which circles downtown Tokyo, and Otemachi subway station—took more than 15 minutes.[3]

Education

As in other countries, homes near good schools and universities command a premium price. If you have young children or are planning to start a family, investigate the availability of daycare places in your target neighborhood. Daycare admissions are managed at the municipal level and cities have different eligibility criteria, depending on the age of the child and the parents' occupation and marital status.

In the spring of 2009, Kawasaki City and Tokyo's Setagaya-ku had long waiting lists for places in government-licensed daycare centers. Midyear admissions are a particular problem in facilities with long waiting lists.[4] See www.i-kosodate.net (Japanese only) for more information.

Machiya

If you are looking for a distinctive home, Kyoto's traditional townhouses (*machiya*) might fit the bill. Machiya are long, narrow wooden houses that combine work and residential spaces. These elegant homes often feature an enclosed garden and are popular with people seeking a slower, relaxed pace. While the number of machiya has been declining, they have been recognized as an important part of Kyoto's architectural heritage and the World Monuments Fund has added these houses to its watch list. For more information, see Kyoto Machiya Resource (www.kyotomachiya.com), the Kyoto Center for Community Collaboration (http://kyoto-machisen.jp/fund) and the Machiya Information Center (www.kyomachiya.net, Japanese only).

City versus suburbs

One of the first choices facing a home buyer is whether to live in the city or the suburbs.

Here are two sample listings taken from the Internet in December 2009. The examples illustrate the costs involved in buying a condominium and the relationship between a property's price and its size, age and distance from central Tokyo. In short, if you are willing to commute for at least one hour each way and live in a slightly older unit and a less-prestigious neighborhood, you can get 90% more space for 11% less money.

Many people choose to live in the city center to avoid Tokyo's crowded commuter trains.

Example No. 1 uses a fixed-rate mortgage, whereas example No. 2 uses a variable-rate mortgage. Both examples use mortgage rates that were current in December 2009. Note that fire and earthquake insurance are not included.

Example No. 1: Downtown Tokyo

This 41-square-meter condominium in central Tokyo's Chuo-ku is a two-minute walk from two popular subway lines, which are five minutes from Tokyo Station. The property is a year old and was built by a well-known developer using reinforced concrete. The unit is on the 13th floor, has a balcony and southern exposure and is on owned rather than leased land.

Purchase	
Price	¥38,000,000
Plus 8% closing costs	3,040,000
Subtotal	41,040,000
Less 10% down payment	−4,104,000
Mortgage amount	**¥36,936,000**

Monthly costs	
Mortgage payment (30-year fixed-rate mortgage @ 2.95%)	¥154,729
Condominium management fee	9,430
Building repair fee	3,270
CATV and Internet fee	2,215
Parking fee	45,000
Taxes (estimated annual tax divided by 12)	16,625
Total	**¥231,269**

Example No. 2: The suburbs

This 78-square-meter condominium is in Tachikawa, in Tokyo's western suburbs. It is a 13-minute walk to the nearest train station, which is a minimum of 45 minutes from Tokyo Station. The property is five years old and is built using reinforced concrete. The unit is on the 3rd floor with a balcony and southern exposure and sits on owned land.

Purchase	
Price	¥33,800,000
Plus 8% closing costs	2,704,000
Subtotal	36,504,000
Less 10% down payment	-3,650,400
Mortgage amount	**¥32,853,600**

Monthly costs	
Mortgage payment (30-year variable-rate mortgage @ 1.2%)	¥108,715
Condominium management fee	7,730
Building repair fee	6,340
Parking fee	13,000
Taxes (estimated annual tax divided by 12)	14,800
Total	**¥150,585**

Rural living

Low prices, abundant fresh air and good quality of life have sparked a renewed interest in Japan's rural areas. If you do not need to commute to the city every day or want to immerse yourself in the Japanese experience, rural living can be attractive. But there are drawbacks.

A rural house and land can be purchased for a few million yen, a price that will seem absurdly low to anyone who experienced the property bubble of the 1980s and early 1990s. Rural prices have followed the national trend, which saw residential prices fall 4.0% for the year ended July 1, 2009, the 18th consecutive year of declines. The drop has been exacerbated by rural depopulation and a decline in the number of farmers. Without a reversal in Japan's immigration policy or a spike in the fertility rate, the rural population will continue to fall. As a result, you will almost certainly sell your property for less than you paid for it.

Falling prices and a shrinking resale market make banks hesitant to lend on rural property. Many foreigner-friendly banks will only lend on urban property. This can make it difficult to finance your purchase and to sell your property when you are ready to move on. In addition, the isolation and quiet that foreigners appreciate is often seen as a negative by local buyers.

Rural economies will suffer if the Hatoyama administration delivers on its plan to cancel dams, highways and other large infrastructure projects, which have been a traditional source of rural jobs. Coupled with the poor financial health of many prefectural and municipal governments, this could cause more hospital, airport and school closures.

There are few international schools in rural areas. Families may have to choose between sending their children to a local school or home-schooling, an increasingly viable option with a high-speed Internet connection.

Physical isolation and the inability to obtain services in English can be an issue if you don't speak Japanese. As in other countries, it takes time for an outsider to gain trust and acceptance in a rural community.

Finally, many rural houses offered at bargain prices are in need of repair, which can be costly and time-consuming. Buyers thinking of changing the use of their land should research this carefully, because the process can be extremely difficult.

Japanese addresses

Japan is divided into 47 prefectures, 43 of which carry the suffix *ken*. The remainder use different suffixes. Hokkaido is a *do*, Osaka and Kyoto are *fu*, while Tokyo is a metropolis (*to*).

Prefectures are subdivided into cities (*shi*) or counties (*gun* or *shicho*). Gun and shicho are further divided into towns (*machi* or *cho*) and villages (*mura* or *son*), which may be split into large sections (*oaza*), sections (*aza*) or small sections (*koaza*).

The 15 largest cities—Chiba, Fukuoka, Hiroshima, Kawasaki, Kitakyushu, Kobe, Kyoto, Nagoya, Osaka, Saitama, Sapporo, Sendai, Shizuoka, Tokyo and Yokohama—are subdivided into wards (*ku*). Ku are further divided into machi or cho, which are separated into city districts (*chome*), city blocks (*banchi*) and building numbers (*go*).

A typical Japanese address (in this example, the Minato Ward Office) is 1-5-25, Shiba-koen, Minato-ku, Tokyo 105-8511, where "1" is the chome number; "5" is the city block number; "25" is the building number; "Shiba-koen" is the town; "Minato" is the ward; and "105-8511" is the postal code.

When written in Japanese, addresses begin with the large (prefecture) and end with the small (building number). When written in English, this order is reversed.

Major thoroughfares, like Tokyo's Yasukuni Dori, have names, but most streets do not. In old neighborhoods, building numbers often reflect the order in which the structures were erected. In newer areas, building numbers may be sequential. Kyoto and Sapporo use variations on the addressing scheme outlined above.

Tokyo includes 23 special wards, 26 cities, three towns, a village and the Izu and Ogasawara islands. Located in the Pacific Ocean, the islands have two towns and seven villages. The Tokyo Metropolitan Area, which is also known as the Greater Tokyo Area, comprises Tokyo and Saitama, Kanagawa and Chiba prefectures.

WHAT TO BUY

In addition to picking an urban, suburban or rural location, home buyers must decide whether they want a new or pre-owned home and choose a detached house or condominium. These decisions are complicated in Japan, where people have a strong preference for new things. This includes homes, which are often viewed as consumer goods.

New and improved

Historically, Japanese homes have had a short life span. Housing is typically demolished after 30 years, versus an average of 55 years in the United States and 77 years in the United Kingdom. Shorter life spans lead to a much smaller market for pre-owned homes: In 2003, used homes represented just 13% of total sales, compared with 78% in the U.S. and 89% in Britain.[1]

Several factors support the preference for new homes. Houses have often been damaged or destroyed by earthquakes, discouraging owners from investing in durable construction. Buildings and land are separate legal entities. Buildings depreciate rapidly, while land does not depreciate at all. Until 2005, tax incentives were offered for new homes but not pre-owned dwellings. Many people continue to subscribe to the idea of "one generation, one home" and demolish houses that are still habitable. Finally, homes where people have died are seen as tainted and are usually demolished and rebuilt.

In 2008, the government introduced initiatives to promote the construction of ultra-long-life houses, including tax incentives, new construction standards that accommodate renovations and upgrades and programs to promote environmentally friendly designs. The environmental benefits of these houses are significant. One study estimated that an ultra-long-life house would produce 21% less CO_2 and 46% less waste than an equivalent series of traditional houses.[2]

As part of the ultra-long-life house program, the government is encouraging home renovations, maintenance and associated record keeping. This is important because the perception of homes as consumable items, coupled with Japan's long working hours and the lack of a do-it-yourself culture, means basic maintenance is often neglected, unnecessarily shortening a building's life span.

Despite these initiatives, there is still a strong bias toward new homes, which are easier to finance and generally offer better energy efficiency than older units. As housing starts, which fell 27.9% in 2009, continue to decline, new homes command a premium price.[3]

New homes are also covered by a 10-year warranty (see "The buying process") and offer superior earthquake resistance. New condominiums are more likely to use vibration dampers and base-isolation devices between the building and its foundation. Base-isolation devices reduce the amount of energy reaching upper floors and limit the damage caused by a tremor. However, tall buildings equipped with these devices tend to sway in high winds and stay in motion longer after an earthquake.[4]

Pre-owned homes

It is possible to find attractively priced used homes, but you must buy carefully. Dates play an important part in the screening process:

- Avoid homes built before national construction standards were tightened in June 1981.

- Dwellings built from 1990 to 1993 can be interesting, because some developers continued to add expensive extras, believing that the market would rebound.

- In April 2000, the Housing Quality Assurance Act (HQAA) took effect. The HQAA includes standards for measuring housing performance (including earthquake resistance), a compulsory 10-year warranty for new homes and a dispute-resolution system for home buyers.[5]

- In October 2009, the Act for Execution of Housing Defect Warranty Liability came into force. Under the act, housing suppliers must buy insurance or participate in a deposit program so that warranties are honored even if the supplier becomes insolvent. The act also strengthened the dispute-resolution system introduced under the HQAA.

One of the biggest advantages to pre-owned homes is that they are often heavily or fully depreciated. A lot with an old building can be worth less than a nearby vacant lot, because the buyer must pay to have the old structure demolished and the debris hauled away. Home builder Sekisui Heim estimates that the demolition of a detached home produces about 40 tonnes of rubble.[6]

Earthquakes

To minimize the likelihood of earthquake-related problems, look for:

- Homes constructed by reputable companies, such as members of Japan's large corporate groupings (*keiretsu*).

- Buildings that have been regularly and properly maintained. Visible damage and water stains suggest that maintenance may be an issue.

- Symmetrical buildings, where the load-bearing walls are evenly distributed.[7]

- Buildings in which walls on upper floors are directly above and supported by walls on lower floors.

- Homes with reinforced concrete foundations or pilings.

- Newer buildings, which are generally more earthquake-resistant than older ones.

You should avoid:

- Neighborhoods near active fault lines.

- Reclaimed land, which is at risk of liquefaction during an earthquake.

- Homes situated on soft sedimentary rock, which amplifies seismic waves during an earthquake. Reclamations and sedimentary rock are common in the Tokyo area.

- Buildings that have been modified or survived a major earthquake or fire. These homes may have suffered structural damage that will not be apparent in a visual inspection.

- Homes with large internal staircases, which can distort the building's structure in an earthquake.

- Wooden homes that have been weakened by termites or rot.[8]

- Condominiums built, inspected or sold by Kimura Construction, Huser Management and E-Homes,[9] all of which were associated with architect Hidetsugu Aneha.[10] For more information, see "Risk factors."

Unlike in other countries, home inspectors are rare in Japan. As a result, it can be difficult to identify problems in a pre-owned home. Older buildings may also use nonstandard fittings, such as odd-sized doors, which can complicate renovation projects. The electrical systems in these buildings may also need to be upgraded to meet modern requirements.

Condominiums

In 2007, there were 5.3 million condominium units in Japan. Known in Japanese as *manshon*, condominiums represent about 70% of the housing built for sale. Condominiums are usually defined as steel-reinforced concrete, steel-framed reinforced concrete or steel-framed buildings that are three stories or taller.

In condominiums, top-floor units, corner units and units with southern exposure command higher prices. This is because:

- South-facing units receive more sunlight in the winter and less in the summer. This makes them warm during the winter and cool during the summer and thus less expensive to heat and cool. This advantage is less evident on lower floors and in densely built complexes that receive less sunshine throughout the year.

- Corner units have fewer adjoining homes, reducing the possibility that noise will be an issue for you and your neighbors. Corner units also enjoy better air circulation and receive more sunlight.

- Top-floor units are further from street noise and have no upstairs neighbors. However, top-floor units can be more expensive to heat and cool if they are improperly insulated.

- The popularity of these units makes them easier to resell.

If you are buying a pre-owned condominium, ask the owners' committee for its annual report, which will include financial projections for the building and the amount of money in the building's repair fund, as well as information about major problems and long-term rehabilitation plans.

You should also ask if the owners' committee intends to raise the monthly building repair fees (*shuzen tsumitate kin*) and if there are plans to retrofit the building to meet new standards, such as the auxiliary brakes on elevators that have been proposed under revisions to the Building Standard Law.[11] Many condominiums will also need new television antennas and distribution systems to accommodate the change from analog to digital terrestrial broadcasts, which is scheduled for July 2011.

Some condominiums—particularly buildings in desirable locations where property taxes are higher and those with extensive facilities—have high condomium management fees (*kanri-hi*). Many buyers overlook these buildings, because they prefer to spend their money on mortgage payments. If you don't mind higher fees, these buildings can sometimes offer an attractive combination of price, amenities and construction and maintenance quality.

Measuring up

Japanese dwellings are described by their size, which can be indicated in square meters; in *jo*, each of which is 180 centimeters by 90 centimeters or about the size of one standard tatami mat; or in *tsubo*, which are about 3.3 square meters.

Homes are also described using the LDK system, where L is the living room, D is the dining room and K is the kitchen. A 1K apartment has one room plus a small kitchen (often comprising a hotplate, a bar fridge and a sink). If the letters LDK appear together, the living room, dining room and kitchen are combined into one room. Therefore, a 3LDK apartment has three rooms, plus a combined living room, dining room and kitchen. A 2DK apartment has two rooms, plus a combined dining room and kitchen.

Older buildings have higher maintenance costs. Condominiums typically need large-scale repairs 10 years after completion and again around the 20-year mark.[12] At about 30 years, most existing buildings need to be rebuilt.[13] Newer buildings are designed and built with a longer life span in mind.

More than 600,000 condominium units in Japan are now over 30 years old, with that figure expected to reach 1 million by 2016.[14] Redevelopment or large-scale rehabilitation of these buildings is difficult. If done on a voluntary basis, it requires a consensus among all of the owners. If done on a legal basis, redevelopment or rehabilitation requires the approval of 80% of the owners. This process is complicated by the advanced age of many owner-occupiers, who may not see the benefit in upgrading the building or want to relocate during the renovations. Tenants renting units in the condominium will also need to be compensated if they are forced to move.

Height restrictions, sunshine laws and plot ratios, which specify a building's total permissible floor space in relation to the size of the plot on which it stands, are also barriers to redevelopment. Buildings that were in compliance with regulations when they were erected in the 1960s and 1970s are exempted from regulations that were enacted after they were completed. But if these buildings are redeveloped, their replacements must comply with new codes that could reduce the building's height or floor space. This is a common problem for condominiums erected before 1981 in major cities.

You can also buy units in government-built condominium complexes called *kodan*. Many of these buildings were constructed to a high standard during the 1960s and 1970s and properly maintained in the meantime. For more information, see the Higashinihon Jutaku Website (www.higashinihonjutaku.co.jp, Japanese only).

If you are considering condominiums from the 1960s and 1970s, watch out for reinforced concrete buildings in which the pipes are embedded in the concrete. Unlike pipes on the outside of the building, embedded plumbing is difficult and expensive to replace.

Leasehold versus freehold

In Japan, land and buildings are separate legal entities[15] and are listed individually in the registry (*tokibo*)[16] at the Legal Affairs Bureau (*houmukyoku*). It is not unusual for a building owned by one person to be erected on land leased from a second person. Buildings on leased land are called leasehold properties, while those on owned land are freehold.

Leasehold condominiums can be purchased at a discount from comparable freehold units. Leasehold detached homes are also available. If you buy a leasehold condominium, you pay a monthly land rental fee in addition to condominium and building repair fees. Monthly rents of ¥10,000–¥30,000 are common, depending on the location, number of units in the building and other factors.

There are significant drawbacks to buying leasehold property:

- Buildings depreciate and have short life spans. Your home may have negative value at the end of the lease if you have to pay the demolition and disposal costs.

- If a fire or earthquake destroys your home, you are left with nothing except the proceeds from any insurance policies you have purchased.

- Lenders may be reluctant to provide a mortgage for leasehold property.

- Owners of leasehold homes spend about 30% less on maintenance than freehold owners, and their homes are less likely to be in sound condition.[17]

- There is no guarantee the landowner will renew your lease, which typically has a 50-year term. Japanese homes last 30–60 years, however, so this is not usually a problem.

Detached homes

In the fiscal year ended March 31, 2009, 424,314 detached houses (*ikkodate*) were built in Japan. Of these, 72% were wooden post-and-beam construction; 11% were wooden 2x4; 3% were wooden prefabricated; 11% were non-wooden prefabricated; and 3% were steel or reinforced concrete.[18]

Detached houses are built by companies ranging from small independent firms, which may only complete a handful of projects each year, to multinational corporations that operate across Japan and sell tens of thousands annually. Smaller builders focus on less expensive post-and-beam and some 2x4 construction. Mitsui Home (www.mitsuihome.co.jp) and Sumitomo Forestry (http://sfc.jp) are the largest builders in the 2x4 category.

Builders such as Asahi Kasei Homes (www.asahi-kasei.co.jp), Daiwa House (www.daiwahouse.co.jp), Misawa Homes (www.misawa.co.jp), PanaHome (www.panahome.jp), Sekisui Heim (www.sekisuiheim.com), Sekisui House (www.sekisuihouse.co.jp) and SxL (www.sxl.co.jp) prefabricate house subassemblies using computerized manufacturing techniques. Subassemblies are built in factories, where they are protected from the weather during the manufacturing process. This helps the builders minimize defects, reduce waste and increase efficiency. The completed subassemblies are then delivered to a building site, where a roof is added and the interior work is completed.

Prices for small, basic single-family homes start at under ¥9 million, excluding land. Homes range from under 60 square meters to over 300 square meters and are usually customized to meet the buyer's requirements. Many large builders will also custom-design homes. The time from contract signing to handover is usually between two and four months.

Builders advertise through exhibitions, show homes, Websites and catalogs, while their homes are sold through dealer networks. In general, builders do not offer financing, but dealers maintain relationships with lenders and help buyers arrange financing. Large builders will often acquire a plot of residential land, which they will subdivide into individual lots. The lots are sold to customers, who agree to buy a home from the builder immediately or at a later date. Customers can also buy a plot of land independently and then ask a builder to erect a house for them (*uri tate*). Builders will also erect houses on a speculative basis and then sell them (*tate uri*).

Large builders often work with quasi-governmental organizations such as the Urban Renaissance Agency (www.ur-net.go.jp) and local government housing corporations. These organizations sell residential land to the builders, which subdivide the land and sell plots to end users as described above. Some of these projects are integrated developments that include schools, shopping malls, condominiums and rental housing.

Japan's leading builders invest heavily in research and development. Their homes are engineered to withstand earthquakes, typhoons and fires, as well as to maintain a healthy indoor environment, with good ventilation, consistent temperatures throughout the home and no emissions of volatile organic compounds. Large builders also work to maximize their homes' energy efficiency and reduce emissions of CO_2 through the installation of photovoltaic cells. Many companies have launched recycling programs that reuse components from demolished homes.

Wooden kit homes, which are known in Japan as log houses, are available through importers such as Lindal Cedar Homes (www.lindal.com; www.lindaljapan.com, Japanese only) and Sweden House (www.swedenhouse.co.jp, Japanese only), which also offer assembly services.

A new development in Kanagawa

A wrong turn helped Jean-Guy Rioux, Jr., and his wife, Noriko, find their new home in a subdivision 90 minutes southwest of Tokyo.

After renting for a decade, in 2000 Jean-Guy and Noriko began searching for a home of their own. A native of Canada, Jean-Guy is an information and communications technology manager who speaks Japanese and has lived in the Tokyo area for nearly two decades. Noriko is a human resources specialist in the pharmaceutical industry.

Jean-Guy and Noriko began their search around Hiratsuka, Kanagawa Prefecture, because Noriko's family lives nearby. The couple looked at houses and vacant lots in the area, but didn't see anything they liked and felt custom building would be too difficult.

"Some real estate agents we spoke to didn't know foreigners could buy property in Japan," says Jean-Guy. "Several looked like yakuza and a few told us that, if we bought their lot, we would have to use a specific construction company to build our home. It wasn't encouraging."

Then, a wrong turn on a Sunday afternoon drive left them in front of a Tokyu Homes (www.tokyu-homes.co.jp, Japanese only) display home. Jean-Guy and Noriko got out of their van and struck up a conversation with a salesman.

"The salesman made it easy for us," notes Jean-Guy. "He understood the tax breaks and incentives that were available and helped us arrange a mortgage."

Two months later, Jean-Guy and Noriko moved into their newly completed home. Situated on a 180-square-meter lot in an 800-home development, the 130-square-meter, two-story detached house has five bedrooms, two of which were converted into a home office. Construction of the development, which comprises five phases, began in 1992.

Jean-Guy describes the home as a Japanese interpretation of a suburban home you'd find in Canada or the United States,

Detached homes are more affordable outside the city center.

but with local touches like a tatami room, a high-technology toilet and an automatic bathtub. The home uses 2x4 construction and includes a sun room and garden, where the couple grows cucumbers, tomatoes, garlic and onions.

Jean-Guy and Noriko made a 50% down payment when they bought the home, which cost approximately ¥56 million, including taxes, fees and incidental expenses. Tokyu Homes helped the couple arrange a 3.5%, 15-year, fixed-rate mortgage from the Government Housing Loan Corporation* for the balance.

In 2005, Jean-Guy and Noriko replaced their mortgage with a 1.95%, five-year, fixed-rate mortgage from Shinsei Bank (www.shinseibank.com). A 1% tax credit from the national government on the outstanding balance of their mortgage meant the couple was effectively paying less than 1% per year to finance their home.

"We looked at six or seven banks, but Shinsei had the best rate," says Jean-Guy. "Shinsei's ATM (automated teller machine) cards work overseas, which was also a plus." While Jean-Guy had banked with Shinsei for more than a year before applying for the mortgage, he didn't think his existing relationship helped his mortgage application.

Nearly a decade after moving in, Jean-Guy and Noriko remain happy with their home. The neighborhood is green and quiet, retaining the suburban feel that the couple wanted. Parks and a public swimming pool are nearby, while frequent bus and train services make it easy to commute to Tokyo or to the nearby cities of Hiratsuka and Odawara.

Jean-Guy and Noriko are also satisfied with the construction quality of their home. They've experienced no significant problems and Tokyu Homes has made regular follow-up visits to fix minor issues, like adjusting door hinges and repairing scratches and dents. In fact, the only negatives the couple have found were the windows, which are double- and not triple-glazed, and that the utility cables are on poles and not buried like they are in newer developments.

*The Government Housing Loan Corporation was succeeded by the Japan Housing Finance Agency, which no longer originates home loans.

Jean-Guy recommends buying from a large developer to eliminate the need to deal with small local real estate agents, whom he feels are not always trustworthy. Buying from a developer also meant the couple did not need to pay a large deposit to a construction company that might become insolvent halfway through the project.

Based on recent sales in the neighborhood, Jean-Guy and Noriko believe the home was a good investment. While the house has depreciated, the value of the land has increased, leaving them in positive territory.

"If you want to make money, buying a condo near a train station in Tokyo, Yokohama or another big city might be a better idea," observes Noriko. "But if you're looking for a home, these developments are a good way to go."

RISK FACTORS

Here are some of the more common risks you may encounter when buying or building a home in Japan. See "Resources" for information about managing these risks.

Antiquities

Japan has over 440,000 registered archeological sites,[1] some of which are believed to be 120,000 years old. As retired professor of archeology and anthropology Charles T. Keally notes on his Website, nearly 70% of Japan is steep mountains so the density of archeological sites is very high on the remaining 30%.[2]

You are required to notify the Agency for Cultural Affairs (www. bunka.go.jp) if you are starting construction in an area known to have buried cultural properties. Maps of archeological sites are available from your ward or city office. If you unearth a relic, you are required to give it to the local chief of police. If the object is believed to be significant, it will then be sent to the local board of education for evaluation. If the owner of the relic is unknown, ownership generally reverts to the prefecture.

Real estate agents are required to disclose the existence of buried antiquities in the explanation of important matters (*juyou jikou setsumeisho*).

Asbestos

A naturally occurring family of minerals known for its tensile strength and resistance to heat, electricity and chemicals, asbestos was imported into Japan from the late 1800s. Inhaling asbestos fibers causes lung cancer, mesothelioma, asbestosis and other diseases. The World Health Organization notes that "there is no evidence for a threshold for the carcinogenic effect of asbestos and that increased cancer risks have been observed in populations exposed to very low levels."[3]

Most people become ill from asbestos through occupational exposure. The decomposition of building materials and asbestos released into the air through renovation and demolition projects also poses a risk.[4] In 1995, the Great Hanshin Earthquake released more than 26 kilograms of the mineral into the air, mainly from insulation and fireproofing in damaged buildings.[5]

Japan was a major user of asbestos in its shipbuilding, petrochemical and pharmaceutical industries and in the manufacture of electrical equipment; automotive clutches and brake pads; and building materials, such as flooring, shingles, water pipes, joint compound, ceiling tiles and wallboard.

Asbestos was also found in vermiculite, a mineral used in thermal insulation and fireproofing and as a potting material for plants. W.R. Grace & Co. produced vermiculite at a mine and milling facility in Libby, Montana, from 1963 to 1990.[6] Vermiculite from the Libby mine—which represented 80% of the global supply—was used in W.R. Grace's Zonolite® attic insulation and early formulations of Monokote® fireproofing.[7] In 2009, asbestos was discovered in Zonolite used in three community centers in Hokkaido and Kagawa Prefecture and in a privately owned building in Tokyo.[8]

Despite a series of international bans that started in Iceland in 1983,[9] Japan allowed the limited use of asbestos as recently as 2006.[10] A report released by the Japan External Trade Organization states that Japan will have to manage approximately one million tonnes of asbestos waste per year between 2008 and 2028.[11]

The extensive use of asbestos, in conjunction with latency periods of up to 40 years for asbestos-related diseases, has caused one expert to call asbestos an "environmental time bomb" for Japan. Kubota Corp. acknowledged that 141 employees died of asbestos-related diseases between 1978 and 2009.[12] The families of dead workers have successfully sued for occupational asbestos exposure[13] and, as of June 2009, 1,855 people had been diagnosed with asbestos-related mesothelioma and 470 with lung cancer.[14]

The Ministry of the Environment (MoE) monitors atmospheric asbestos concentrations at 149 points in 50 areas. In a report for fiscal 2008, ended March 31, 2009, the MoE stated, "The results do not indicate hazardous levels of asbestos either in the atmosphere or in the areas bordering demolition work sites, except for some areas inside those demolition sites."[15]

Despite this reassurance, it would be wise to exercise caution if you are buying an old building; if you live in a neighborhood where old buildings are being demolished or renovated; or if you are buying property in former industrial areas of Osaka,[16] which has a history of manufacturing asbestos textiles, or Kure, where asbestos was used in shipyards and cement pipe factories.[17]

Real estate agents are required to disclose the existence of asbestos in the explanation of important matters.

Burakumin

Some 2 million–3 million Japanese are descendants of the *burakumin*, people who performed "unclean" jobs in slaughterhouses, tanneries and morgues during the Tokugawa period (1600–1867).[18] These workers and their families were treated as outcasts and segregated in communities known as *buraku*, of which 3,000–6,000 remain.

Buraku are generally found in undesirable locations, such as flood-prone areas and slopes. They exist in Kobe, Osaka, Kyoto and Tokyo, while Hokkaido and Okinawa are the only prefectures without these enclaves. Today, buraku are often indistinguishable from other districts. Clusters of businesses selling products manufactured from leather are often the only clue to a neighborhood's past.

Property prices in buraku are generally lower and public works projects often take longer than in other precincts, so Japanese buyers avoid these areas. Lists of buraku are also reported to be circulating on the Internet.

Official discrimination against burakumin ended in the Meiji era (1868–1912), but burakumin routinely face prejudice today. Families will hire private investigators to check the family register (*koseki*) of prospective spouses to ensure they have no burakumin ancestors; landlords are unwilling to rent to burakumin; and major corporations will not hire them.[19]

Buraku are not shown on modern maps, although they can be found on old ones. In 2009, Google sparked a controversy in Japan, when it added historical maps showing buraku to the Google Earth service. After complaints were received, Google removed the offending references. The historical maps, which may eventually be returned to their original condition, can be viewed online at www.davidrumsey.com.

Death

In Japan, death doesn't mix well with real estate. Large discounts apply to properties where there has been a murder, suicide, natural death, rape or other violent crime. With Japan's aging population and the number of deaths reaching a postwar high of over 1.15 million in 2008, this is going to be an ongoing problem.

Real estate agents are required to disclose deaths and violent crimes in the explanation of important matters. After two title transfers or two years, the death doesn't have to be disclosed to a prospective buyer.

If the death occurred inside a condominium unit, only the person buying that unit must be told. But if the death occurred in a common area, like a lobby or parking lot, everyone in the building must be notified. Locations where fatal fires, bloody battles or wartime executions occurred are suspect. Properties near cemeteries and crematoria are also unpopular.

This can lead to elaborate charades, like corpses not being officially declared dead until they reach the hospital, to prevent a property from being tainted. It also poses a dilemma for real estate agents, who must choose between telling a prospective buyer about a death early in the process (and potentially scaring them off) or waiting until the explanation of important matters.

Agents selling property to non-Japanese buyers may feel that they can safely omit information about a death. And while it may not bother you to live in a home where someone has died, it could unsettle family members and reduce your home's resale value. Talking to your prospective neighbors and asking the real estate agent directly may be a wise move, particularly if a property seems unusually inexpensive.

Defective design and construction

In November 2005, after an investigation by the Ministry of Land, Infrastructure, Transport and Tourism (MLIT), an architect (*kenchikushi*) named Hidetsugu Aneha was discovered to have falsified design data for 21 condominiums and hotels. Ultimately, 99 buildings, mainly in Tokyo, Kanagawa and Chiba prefectures, were affected.[20] Many of the structures, the designs for which had been approved by government and private-sector inspectors, were found to have less than half the earthquake resistance specified by the Building Standard Law and had to be rebuilt or demolished. Despite the Housing Quality Assurance Act (HQAA), which requires developers to provide a 10-year warranty on new homes, several companies declared bankruptcy, leaving hundreds of buyers with uninhabitable homes and unpaid mortgages. The government provided some financial support to individual buyers, and in December 2006 Aneha was sentenced to five years in prison and a ¥1.8 million fine.

In June 2009, the Fukuoka District Court dismissed a ¥120 million lawsuit against Japan ERI, a building inspection company that had certified design calculations for Arc Inn Kurosaki that had been fabricated by Aneha. The presiding judge ruled that because Japan ERI had used government-authorized software to evaluate the hotel's structural data, it was not guilty of a breach of duty.[21]

For home buyers, some good has come from the Aneha affair. Amendments to the Building Standard Law now require that an expert review the structural calculations for reinforced concrete buildings over 20 meters in height. Interim inspections are required for apartment buildings that are three stories or taller and work cannot continue until the building has passed the inspection.[22] Architects must participate in professional education programs and practitioners who are guilty of professional misconduct can now be fined, imprisoned and named.

Another important outcome was the 2007 passage of the Act for Execution of Defect Warranty Liability. An amendment to the HQAA, the act requires developers to buy insurance or participate in a deposit program, so that buyers will be covered by a 10-year warranty even if the developer becomes insolvent.

Under the HQAA, dispute resolution bodies that incorporate local bar associations help home owners resolve warranty-related conflicts with developers and contractors. The Center for Housing Renovation and Dispute Settlement Support (www.chord.or.jp) supports the bar associations, gathers statistics and information and provides Japanese-language telephone assistance to home owners.

Earthquakes

Earthquakes present several threats to people and property, including embankments collapsing and liquefaction of reclaimed land, damage to buildings and other structures caused by earthquakes and subsequent fires, the release of hazardous materials such as asbestos into the environment and tsunami-related destruction. After a major earthquake, buildings may be uninhabitable; transportation, utilities and other key infrastructure may fail; and essential services may be interrupted.

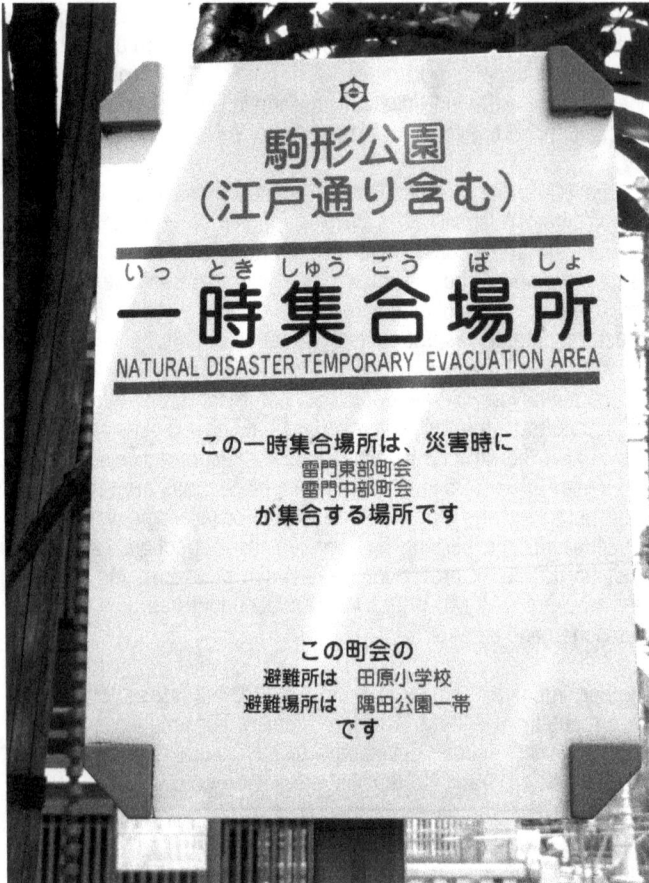

駒形公園
（江戸通り含む）

いっ　とき　しゅうごう　ば　しょ
一時集合場所

NATURAL DISASTER TEMPORARY EVACUATION AREA

この一時集合場所は、災害時に
雷門東部町会
雷門中部町会
が集合する場所です

この町会の
避難所は　田原小学校
避難場所は　隅田公園一帯
です

Cities throughout Japan maintain evacuation areas for use in natural disasters.

Japan is a seismically active country, where earthquakes are a daily occurrence. Most are minor, although the Great Kanto Earthquake, which killed 140,000 people in 1923, and the Great Hanshin Earthquake (GHE), which killed over 6,400 and resulted in losses of ¥12 trillion in 1995, are notable exceptions.

After the GHE, the government established the Headquarters for Earthquake Research Promotion (HERP), a multiagency body charged with preparing Japan for a major earthquake. In a 2006 report, HERP estimated that, within 30 years, there was a 70% chance of Tokyo being struck by a magnitude 7 earthquake that could cause ¥112 trillion in damage and result in up to 11,000 deaths.[23] HERP also estimated that there is an 87% chance of a magnitude 8 earthquake occurring in the Tokai region by 2040,[24] which could cause ¥37 trillion in damage and 10,000 deaths.[25] In addition to their local impact, earthquakes of this intensity would rock the global financial system as the Japanese government and the nation's banks and businesses repatriated their overseas investments to fund the reconstruction effort.

At 7.3 on the Japan Meteorological Agency scale, the Great Hanshin Earthquake was the most costly and lethal earthquake in modern Japanese history. The GHE also demonstrated the importance of revisions to national building standards that took effect on June 1, 1981. Of 923 buildings surveyed in central Kobe after the GHE, 35% of those built before 1971 collapsed or were seriously damaged, 40% had moderate or minor damage and 25% had slight or no damage. For buildings constructed between 1972 and 1981, the statistics were 12%, 31% and 57%, respectively. But only 8% built after 1982 were seriously damaged, with 17% incurring moderate damage and 75% sustaining slight or no damage.[26]

Japan's building standards are designed to achieve two goals. In a moderate earthquake, up to about 5 on the Japanese scale, the building should suffer little or no structural damage and still be safe for occupancy. In a stronger earthquake, the building should not collapse and there should be no casualties as a result of structural failure. This is important because 88% of the fatalities in the GHE were due to collapsing buildings.[27]

Since the GHE, there have been several amendments to the building standards, including measures to promote seismic retrofitting of public facilities, such as apartment buildings, schools, hospitals and shopping centers. Programs have also been introduced to encourage seismic assessments and upgrades of detached homes and condominiums, with subsidies of up to 66% for improvements to properties that are adjacent to emergency transportation or evacuation routes.

Unfortunately, because retrofitting is not mandatory, the earthquake resistance of many older properties has not been enhanced.[28] In 2003, about 11.5 million of Japan's 53 million dwellings did not meet modern earthquake resistance standards.[29]

Economic problems

In 2008, more than 3,000 construction companies and 425 property firms declared bankruptcy in Japan. Notable failures included Urban Corp., C's Create Co., Creed Corp. and Toshin Housing Co. The trend continued in 2009 with the collapse of Anabuki Construction Inc., Azel Corp., Japan General Estate Co., Joint Corp., Pacific Holdings

Co. and others. The fragile state of the real estate and construction sectors means you should investigate your counterparty's financial stability before signing a contract or paying a deposit.

The global recession that began in 2008 also hurt Japanese workers. The average annual pay for private-sector employees fell a record 1.7% in fiscal 2008, to ¥4.29 million, including salary, allowances and bonus. Average bonuses dropped 6%, to ¥646,000, in fiscal 2008 and one worker in four earned ¥3 million or less. Rising unemployment, which reached a post–World War II high of 5.7% in July 2009, is causing an increase in mortgage defaults. That same month, 7,229 properties were auctioned at courts throughout Japan, a 70% increase from 2008, and there has been speculation that canceled or reduced bonuses could drive already stretched home owners into bankruptcy.

Given the current deflationary environment, anyone buying investment property should plan for the possibility of rent reductions. This is especially true for niche markets, such as expatriate apartments. In an informal survey by the U.S.-based National Association of Independent Landlords, 32% of respondents said they had lowered rents in the 18 months ending in October 2009.

Fire

Detached homes in Japan are frequently made of wood and built close together. This makes fire a serious threat, especially after an earthquake. The Fire and Disaster Management Agency estimates there are about 30,000 house fires in Japan each year. In fiscal 2005, 1,559 people died in house fires.

Fire insurance is a standard condition for a mortgage and the Fire Defense Law stipulates that fire alarms incorporating heat sensors or smoke detectors must be installed in homes built after June 1, 2006. Homes built before that date must have fire alarms installed by 2011, although many local governments have set earlier deadlines, which can be obtained from your local fire department. In Tokyo, fire alarms must be installed in all homes by April 1, 2010.[30]

Fire protection zones and quasi fire protection zones can be found along main roads. Buildings in these locations must meet higher fire resistance standards than those in other areas.[31]

Foreign exchange risk

If you operate in yen and a second currency, you'll need to manage your foreign exchange (forex) risk to ensure that a change in the value of the yen doesn't increase your costs or decrease your income. For example, it was difficult to rent ski chalets in Niseko to Australian tourists after the value of the Australian dollar fell against the yen in late 2008, causing the price of a Japanese ski holiday to nearly double in Australian-dollar terms.

If you buy a Japanese property with a mortgage denominated in a currency other than yen, a strengthening yen can increase the loan-to-value ratio of your mortgage. If this happens, the lender may demand additional collateral or require you to make additional payments.

Changes in forex rates can also work in your favor. If the yen strengthens, for example, you could sell a property whose yen value has remained constant and take a profit on the currency appreciation without incurring capital gains tax in Japan.

It is possible to hedge your forex exposure using forward contracts and other instruments, although the cost of the hedge may outweigh the benefits for smaller transactions.

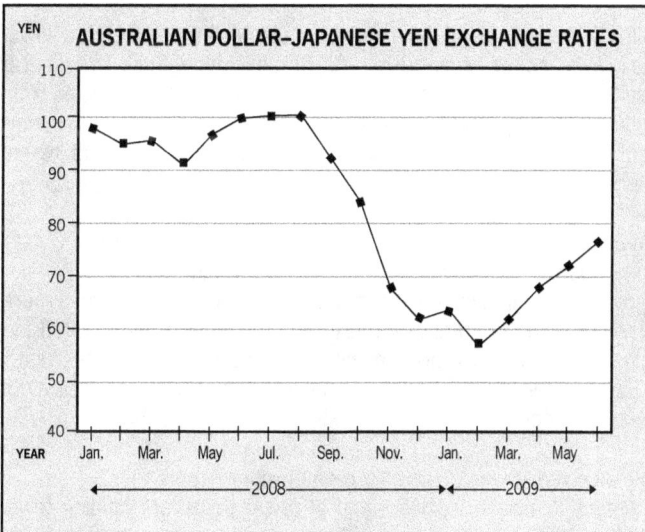

AUSTRALIAN DOLLAR–JAPANESE YEN EXCHANGE RATES

Higher interest rates

The Bank of Japan has maintained a low interest rate policy since 1999, making home ownership more accessible for many people. However, there is no guarantee that this policy will continue.

While many economists cite deflation as their primary short-term concern, qualitative easing in the United States and elsewhere may spark inflationary pressure in the years ahead. That, in turn, may cause central banks, including the Bank of Japan, to raise interest rates.

The withdrawal of credit is a related threat. While Niseko appears to have avoided this problem, in 2009 overseas buyers in Bulgaria, Dubai, Florida and Spain were trapped when banks stopped lending. Without mortgages, secondary market prices plunged by as much as 75%.[32]

Local service reductions

In July 2009, the National Governors' Association announced that the financial crisis had escalated to the point where it was doubtful whether local governments could continue to deliver essential public services.[33] One municipality, Yubari in Hokkaido, declared bankruptcy with debts of more than ¥32 billion.[34]

All 47 prefectural governments announced that they expect lower tax revenues for fiscal 2009, with 38 anticipating their largest-ever declines.[35] Revenue shortfalls, coupled with smaller subsidies from the national government and spending increases needed to support an aging population, are forcing many local governments to cut services.

In January 2009, financial difficulties caused the closure of a 400-bed hospital in Choshi, Chiba Prefecture,[36] and in July the national government announced the first-ever closure of a public airport. The airport is operated by the town of Teshikaga, which cited low passenger numbers and its own financial problems for the decision.[37] Hard-pressed municipalities are also reducing long-term care for elderly people.[38]

Service reductions could also prompt more people to leave smaller centers, fueling a vicious circle of fewer taxpayers funding fewer services. Obviously, this would not be good for property values.

Megaprojects

The noise, dirt and disruption that accompany a megaproject can be stressful and diminish the value of your property. In the Tokyo area, several megaprojects are either in the planning stages or are under way, including the 634-meter Tokyo Sky Tree in Sumida-ku, a proposed ¥1.3 trillion magnetic levitation (Maglev) train line between Narita and Haneda airports and a ¥4 trillion plan to bury 50 kilometers of expressways 60 meters below ground that was presented to Tokyo Governor Shintaro Ishihara in April 2009. The MLIT has also approved a ¥1.5 trillion program for a 16-kilometer underground extension of Tokyo's Gaikan Expressway, as well as large highway projects in Aichi, Yamagata and Ibaraki prefectures.

Megaprojects are usually launched with a major publicity campaign, so watch for television and newspaper coverage and check your city's Website.

Nuclear accidents

Japan has 54 nuclear reactors in Aomori, Ehime, Fukui, Fukushima, Hokkaido, Ibaraki, Ishikawa, Kagoshima, Miyagi, Niigata, Saga, Shimane and Shizuoka. One new reactor is under construction and 13 are being planned. With the exception of a power plant near Kaminoseki, Yamaguchi, the new reactors will be built in prefectures with existing nuclear facilities. A nuclear fuel reprocessing plant in Tokaimura, Ibaraki, is in operation and a plant in Rokkasho, Aomori, has been undergoing commissioning since March 2006.

About 30% of Japan's electricity is generated from nuclear sources. This is set to grow to at least 40% by 2017.[39] Some of the increase is expected to come from "uprating," a process where existing equipment is upgraded without large-scale construction or long shutdowns.

Japan's nuclear power industry has experienced several serious accidents, including a 1995 fire and nonradioactive sodium leak at the Monju fast-breeder reactor in Tsuruga, Fukui; a 1997 fire at a waste bitumenization facility in Tokaimura; a 1999 criticality (uncontrolled nuclear chain reaction) accident at a fuel plant in Tokaimura; a 2004 nonradioactive steam leak in Mihama, Fukui; and a radioactive leak and fire at a power station in Kashiwazaki, Niigata, after an earthquake in 2007.[40] Several of these accidents resulted in fatalities and there have been numerous less serious incidents.

There have also been questions about the industry's transparency. A 1999 criticality accident at the Shika-1 reactor in Ishikawa was not reported to the Nuclear and Industrial Safety Agency until 2007.[41] Allegations of data falsification in 2002 resulted in the Tokyo Electric Power Company shutting down its 17 reactors for safety inspections.

Pandemics

Global influenza outbreaks in 1918, 1957/8 and 1968/9 killed more than 50 million people and some scientists believe that we are overdue for a new pandemic. Influenza is spread by coughing and sneezing and is usually most lethal for the young and old. Japan's crowded commuter trains, growing number of elderly people and overstretched medical system mean an influenza pandemic could have devastating consequences. See the World Health Organization (www.who.int) for more information.

Sick house syndrome

Sick house syndrome (SHS or *shikkuhausu* as it is known in Japanese) is a group of nonspecific symptoms that includes headaches; coughing; irritation of the eyes, nose, throat or skin; dizziness; nausea; difficulty concentrating; and fatigue. It is similar to sick building syndrome, but occurs inside dwellings instead of offices and other public facilities. There is no standard clinical definition for sick building syndrome or SHS but people suffering from either condition usually feel better shortly after they leave the building.

A definitive cause for SHS has not been identified, but it is associated with indoor air pollution, particularly from the volatile organic compounds (VOCs) that are found in adhesives, furniture, wall coverings, paint, flooring, wood products, solvents and cleaning solutions, pesticides and many other products.[42] The Ministry of Health, Labour and Welfare has established guidelines for indoor air levels of 13 VOCs, including toluene, xylene and formaldehyde, and has set a guideline for total VOC levels of 400 micrograms per cubic meter of indoor air.[43]

Because VOCs are used in construction materials, SHS is common in new and newly renovated homes, especially dwellings that have been sealed to increase their energy efficiency. SHS has also been linked to biological contaminants such as mold, bacteria, viruses and pollen and is exacerbated by inadequate ventilation and poor building maintenance.[44] "The Rule of 1,000," which states that pollutants released indoors are 1,000 times more likely to be inhaled than those released outdoors, suggests that even small quantities of these agents can have a large impact indoors.[45]

Airborne chemicals can be removed via physisorption with activated charcoal, porous ceramics and natural fibers; by chemisorption using organic and inorganic compounds; and through decomposition using photocatalysts, negative ions and other techniques. Commercial products, such as electronic air cleaners and passive air cleaning boards that use manganese dioxide to convert formaldehyde into water and carbon dioxide, are also available, as are colorimetric detectors that indicate the presence of formaldehyde.[46]

Developmental, physiological and other factors mean that children are potentially more susceptible to SHS and other forms of environmental chemical exposure than adults.[47] Homemakers and other people who spend a great deal of time at home are also at risk.

Psychosocial factors such as stress and anxiety can play a role in SHS, and some researchers have questioned whether SHS (and related conditions such as multiple chemical sensitivity and idiopathic environmental intolerance) is a panic attack triggered by exposure to "chemical" smells.[48]

However, SHS is widely recognized in Japan and covered by Japanese health insurance.[49] In the first ruling of its kind, in October 2009 the Tokyo District Court ordered developer Dia Kensetsu Co. to pay ¥36.6 million in damages to a woman who developed SHS after moving into one of the company's condominiums.[50]

On July 1, 2003, the Building Standard Law was amended to address SHS. The use of materials containing chlorpyrifos (a chemical used in insecticides and termiticides) in buildings with habitable rooms was banned. Construction materials—including plywood, medium-density fiberboard (MDF), particleboard, laminates, wallpaper, adhesives and thermal insulation—were divided into four groups, based on the amount of formaldehyde they emit. Products in group 1 were banned; those in groups 2 and 3 may be used in limited areas; and products in group 4 can be used without restriction. In addition, the 2003 amendments made the installation of mechanical ventilation systems mandatory in all buildings. Ventilation and formaldehyde-emission specifications were also introduced for attics, crawl spaces, storerooms and similar areas.[51]

Indoor air quality is also covered by the Housing Quality Assurance Act, which was enacted in 2000, and the Japan Housing Performance Indication Standards (JHPIS), which came into effect in 2004. English translations of the HQAA, JHPIS and Building Standard Law can be purchased from the Building Center of Japan (www.bcj.or.jp).

Soil and water pollution

According to *Environmental Finance* magazine, over one-third of former manufacturing sites in Japan have contaminated soil.[52] The Ministry of the Environment estimates 113,000 hectares of land valued at over ¥43 trillion are contaminated,[53] and more than two-thirds of the sites identified in a 2007 MoE survey were located in metropolitan areas.

The MoE classifies hazardous substances into three categories: Class 1 is volatile organic compounds, such as benzene, carbon tetrachloride and trichloroethylene; Class 2 comprises heavy metals including lead, arsenic, cadmium, chromium and mercury; and Class 3 is polychlorinated biphenyls (PCBs) and agrichemicals.[54]

Metal and semiconductor manufacturers, laundries and dry cleaners, and chemical and electrical equipment factories were among the worst sources of industrial pollution. Contaminants typically include VOCs, heavy metals or a combination of the two.

These contaminants seep into groundwater, which is often a source of tap water. The suspected carcinogen trichloroethylene has been found in the groundwater of cities and towns in Chiba, Fukui, Hyogo, Kanagawa, Shiga, Tochigi and Yamagata prefectures, among others.[55] Trichloroethylene concentrations of up to 8,000 parts per billion have been recorded, far above the maximum 30 parts per billion specified by the government.[56]

Contamination is also a problem in Tokyo. In 2008, soil under the proposed new site for the Tsukiji fish market in Toyosu, Koto-ku, was found to contain 43,000 times the allowable amount of the carcinogen benzene.[57] Benzene in nearby groundwater was 10,000 times higher than the legal limit of 10 parts per billion.

About 59,000 tonnes of polychlorinated biphenyls were manufactured in Japan between 1954 and 1972, mainly for use in electrical equipment. Importing and manufacturing PCBs, which are suspected carcinogens, have been outlawed since 1974, but large quantities remain in storage throughout Japan because of public opposition to the construction of treatment facilities. According to the Japan Environmental Safety Corporation (JESCO), a government-owned company responsible for PCB waste treatment, "most of the banned PCB products are still stored at their holder's sites, and fear of damage to the environment caused by leakage, misplacement or dumping of the wastes is still a crucial issue." JESCO operates five PCB treatment facilities, including one in Koto-ku.[58]

The Law Concerning Special Measures Against PCB Waste requires that all PCB-contaminated waste be destroyed before July 14, 2016.[59] The transport and destruction of PCBs and remediation of contaminated sites will attract considerable public attention as the deadline approaches.

Property owned by small companies is frequently affected because the lots are smaller, the contamination affects a large proportion of the land and the owners often lack the money to pay for remediation, which can cost ¥50,000 per cubic meter of soil. In addition, some industrial sites were converted to residential use in the 1960s and 1970s, before there was much awareness of, or testing for, soil contamination.

Landowners typically don't want to test for soil contamination because of high remediation costs, the popular preference for excavation and removal of contaminated soil (instead of less expensive containment measures) and the stigma associated with owning contaminated land. In a 2003 survey by the Japan Real Estate Institute and Meikai University Graduate School of Real Estate Sciences of residential buyers' attitudes toward contaminated land, just 9% of respondents said they would be willing to buy land or an apartment on a site that had been remediated. Nearly two-thirds would not purchase a property if there was a history of soil contamination.[60]

Real estate agents are required to disclose soil contamination in the explanation of important matters. It is also worth checking the neighborhood for so-called brownfield sites, which are former industrial zones that have not been remediated, usually because the land's low value makes the cleanup cost uneconomical. The presence of these sites can reduce the value of nearby land, especially if there are concerns about contaminants entering the groundwater.

According to the Soil Contamination Countermeasures Act (Act No. 53 of 2002), when a facility using hazardous substances is abandoned, the owner must commission an authorized company to investigate whether the soil is contaminated. The government can also initiate an investigation if a site is believed to constitute a public health hazard.[61] Prefectural governments maintain lists of contaminated sites, which remain on the list until the authorities are satisfied that the site no longer poses a threat.

Tax increases

Japan's soaring public debt, growing social security spending and declining tax revenues mean tax increases are a distinct possibility.

At 174%, Japan's ratio of gross government debt to gross domestic product is the highest of the Group of Seven countries.[62] Social security spending now represents about half of general expenditures and in June 2009 the government said it would abandon a program to trim growth in social security spending by ¥220 billion each year up to fiscal 2011.[63]

Lower corporate and personal tax remittances during the recession led to a ¥9.3 trillion tax shortfall in fiscal 2008,[64] while net corporate tax receipts in the first half of fiscal 2009 were minus ¥1.3 trillion, after refunds of tax prepayments. It was the first time since 1960 that first-half corporate tax receipts were negative.[65]

The Japan Business Federation (Nippon Keidanren) and the government's National Council on Social Security have proposed raising Japan's consumption tax to 10%–11% in 2015 and 17%–18% in 2025 to finance social spending. Higher taxes are unlikely to help consumer confidence or the economy in general.

Termites

Dry-wood termites (*Incisitermes minor*) can be found in 24 of Japan's 47 prefectures, including Tokyo. These insects, which can destroy a wooden house, are believed to have arrived in lumber imported from the United States.

Dry-wood termites are more mobile, harder to exterminate and immune to the chemicals used to kill the subterranean termites that are commonly found in Japan. Dry-wood termites often inhabit roofing materials, which should be treated with termiticidal chemicals before construction.[66] If you are considering the purchase of a pre-owned wooden house, call for a termite inspection if you see small piles of frass (termite excrement).

Typhoons, floods and landslides

Japan is a wet country. The average annual rainfall ranges from 1,127 millimeters in Sapporo to 1,466 in Tokyo and 2,279 in Kagoshima. On average, more than 26 cyclones of tropical storm strength or greater form in the seas around Japan each year, usually between July and October, with three making landfall. Japan also has many short, steep rivers that contribute to flash floods.

Nearly half the population and three-quarters of the nation's assets are located in flood-prone alluvial lowlands.[67] To protect them, national, prefectural and local governments have built flood-control structures including pumping stations, concrete river embankments and dams. These structures have greatly reduced the intensity and frequency of floods and enabled development in previously unusable areas. But by concentrating the runoff and shortening the period between the rainfall and peak water discharge, these structures can create new risks, particularly when embankments fail or rainfall exceeds a waterway's design specifications.

Typhoon Isewan (also known as Typhoon Vera), which struck the Tokai area on September 26, 1959, was the worst typhoon in Japanese history. With a storm surge of 3.45 meters and winds of over 163 kilometers per hour, the storm left over 5,000 people dead or missing and nearly 39,000 injured. It washed away over 4,600 homes, totally or partially destroyed 160,000 and submerged more than 190,000.[68]

Typhoon Isewan resulted in the passage of the Disaster Measures Basic Law, which specified the responsibilities of national, prefectural and local governments. It also prompted the construction of an extensive network of sea walls, water gates and other structures to protect Ise, Osaka and Tokyo bays.

Tokyo is particularly vulnerable to tsunamis, storm surges and rising sea levels. About 20% of the land in the city's 23 wards is below the normal high-water mark and 9.3 million people live in the basin of the Arakawa River, which runs through the city.[69] The Central Disaster Management Council estimates that if a major typhoon caused the Arakawa River to burst its banks, 97 subway[70] stations would be flooded and thousands of people killed.[71]

High levels of rainfall, mountainous terrain and frequent earthquakes make Japan susceptible to landslides. In 1792, between 15,000 and 16,000 people in Shimabara City were killed by falling debris and the resulting tsunami in what remains the world's most deadly landslide. A 35-year study showed that landslides occurred in Japan every year between 1967 and 2002, resulting in almost 3,300 deaths—more fatalities than earthquakes in most years of the study. Landslides cause an estimated US$4 billion–$6 billion in damage annually.[72]

Low-lying areas and land near rivers, canals and other waterways are at particular risk from floods. In the absence of physical clues, names that include words like basin (*bonchi*), marsh (*numa*), ditch (*mizo*), channel (*suido*) or valley (*tani*) may suggest that a neighborhood is vulnerable to flooding.[73]

Real estate agents are required to disclose flood and landslide risks in the explanation of important matters.

The yakuza

Unlike the triads, mafia and other criminal groups that are organized as secret societies, the yakuza (also known as *boryokudan*) are both visible and legal in Japan. At the end of 2007, the National Police Agency estimated that the 21 officially designated boryokudan groups had a total membership of over 84,000 full- and part-time members.[74]

Yakuza gangs have a history of maintaining relationships with political and business leaders. These relationships facilitated their involvement in public works projects, where protection, bid rigging, trucking, waste disposal and managing labor relations on building sites became important sources of yakuza revenues.

In the 1980s, the boryokudan became active in Japan's booming stock and real estate markets, often buying property with loans they were confident would never be repaid. The yakuza also expanded beyond their traditional, vice-based businesses into debt collection, corporate extortion (*sokaiya*) and bankruptcy management services.

The enactment of the Law Concerning Prevention of Unjust Acts by Boryokudan in 1992 made it illegal for designated boryokudan gangs to engage in extortion and intimidation and gave the authorities a greater range of powers with which to prosecute them. As a result, the yakuza accelerated their diversification into new businesses, including investments in real estate agencies and construction companies.

The yakuza also offer property-related services such as mediating real estate disputes and land-sharking (*jiage*), a process in which small landowners are intimidated into selling their property so that it can be incorporated into a larger development.[75]

Property remains a profitable business for the yakuza. Using the tenant-protection provisions in Japanese law, the yakuza employ professional squatters (*senyuya*) to occupy property. Through senyuya, the yakuza enjoy rent-free use of commercial and residential property; purchase real estate at below-market prices after they scare off other prospective buyers and then resell it at a profit; and collect payoffs for vacating occupied property.[76]

The yakuza focus on everything from working-class residential neighborhoods to upmarket commercial and entertainment districts, such as Roppongi in Tokyo. Wealthy areas are often preferred for their prestige and the residents' ability to pay. While the yakuza's primary targets are private owners, they can also be found in public housing estates.

Having gang members as neighbors can reduce a property's rental and resale values and cause stress for you and your family. There is also the remote but real possibility of being caught in the crossfire between warring gangs.

Police boxes, or *koban*, are a common sight throughout Japan.

As a result, checking for yakuza involvement should be part of your due diligence procedures. Start by walking around the neighborhood and looking for the telltale signs: black Mercedes-Benz and Lexus sedans driven by hard-looking men with punch-permed hair, tattoos and missing digits. Consulting local merchants, prospective neighbors and officers in the local police box (*koban*) and nearest police station may also provide useful information, although these inquiries will need to be made in Japanese. The National Center for the Elimination of Boryokudan (www1a.biglobe.ne.jp/boutsui/index2.htm, Japanese only) may also be helpful.

You should also check the credentials of your real estate agent, advises Jake Adelstein, the author of *Tokyo Vice: An American Reporter on the Police Beat in Japan* and a consultant specializing in antisocial forces and corporate malfeasance in Japan.[77] Adelstein says that in 2005 the Tokyo Metropolitan Police Department identified over 1,000 yakuza-run companies in Greater Tokyo, 170 of which were real estate firms.

If you're working with a smaller real estate firm, Adelstein recommends you check with the local government—in Tokyo you can visit www.takken.metro.tokyo.jp (Japanese only)—to ensure the company is licensed to conduct real estate transactions. In addition, Adelstein says,"You should also see if the firm has a home page and have someone fluent in Japanese check it out. I recommend that in all cases you get a copy of the firm's registration, which can be obtained through the Ministry of Justice, and see how long they have been in business and what their capital is currently. Look for huge fluctuations in capital, failure to update the registry every two years, and frequent changes in personnel, company name and location. All these things might suggest a real estate firm doing dubious business."

Adelstein also notes that you can add an organized crime exclusionary clause to the sale and purchase agreement. This clause will nullify the contract if parties involved in the transaction are connected to organized crime or if gang members are occupying the property. Enforcing the clause, however, may be difficult.

These measures should help you avoid buying a yakuza-linked property. But what if the yakuza moves into your building or neighborhood? Recently, community groups in Tokyo's Minato and Toshima wards and in Kurume City, Kyushu, have used injunctions to evict gangs from their neighborhoods. In the past, most people would either try to ignore their new neighbors, pay them to move out or sell their property, usually at a loss.

If the yakuza are aware that you are unhappy with their presence, they may offer to leave in exchange for an exorbitant "moving fee." However, Adelstein warns that if the yakuza ask for a moving fee, they will expect to be paid. Obtaining expert advice, either from a lawyer specializing in yakuza-related issues or from an adviser like Adelstein, may be worthwhile.

Zoning

In Japan, existing buildings generally do not have to be rebuilt to comply with new regulations. However, new rules can make it difficult to redevelop a property or build a new home. Changes to the shadow restrictions (*nichiei kisei*), which prevent a new structure from blocking sunlight from reaching an existing building, make it uneconomical to redevelop some condominiums, because the new building will have to be smaller than the one it replaces.

Similar problems can be encountered with setbacks, which specify the minimum distance between a building and the roadway, especially if the road was widened since the building was erected. Height restrictions (*zettai takasa no seigen*), the building coverage ratio (*kenpei ritsu*) and the floor-area ratio (*youseki ritsu*) can also cause problems.[78]

FINANCE

MORTGAGES

Mortgages, which are also known as home loans or housing loans, are available in Japan through city, regional, trust and online banks; finance companies; and foreign banks.* Most mortgages are sold through direct channels, such as bank branches, rather than through intermediaries.

The Bank of Japan's low interest rate policy has kept mortgage rates affordable. In December 2009, variable-rate mortgages were available from 1.20% per annum, while 30-year fixed-rate mortgages were 2.95%.

In 2006, about 15% of new mortgages were variable rate; 69% were hybrids in which the interest rate floats after an initial fixed period, typically 1, 3, 5, 7 or 10 years; and 16% were fixed rate. Variable-rate mortgages—where the interest rate is reviewed daily, monthly, biannually or annually—generally offer the lowest interest rates, while borrowers pay a premium for the security of a fixed rate for the duration of the mortgage.

Reverse mortgages, which allow elderly people to use their home as security for a nonrecourse loan that is repaid when the home is sold after the borrower and his spouse die, are not common in Japan. Deflation, limited sales data, opaque valuation methods and Japan's underdeveloped credit reporting industry make it difficult for lenders to accurately price these loans. In 2008, Japan's reverse mortgage market was about 1% the size of the U.S. market.

Mortgage repayment schedules can be tailored to the annual or semiannual bonuses that many workers receive. It is common for borrowers to have a modest payment for 10 or 11 months of the year with a large payment in June and/or December when bonuses are paid.

*Interest rates and product and service details change frequently. See lenders' Websites for current information.

You can qualify for a mortgage with two years of continuous employment and an annual income of ¥2 million. If you are self-employed, lenders require two to three years of operating history and profitability. However, these numbers are bare minimums.

In Japan, most residential mortgages are recourse loans. If you default, the lender can foreclose on and force the sale of the mortgaged property. The foreclosure process can take a year or more. If the sale proceeds do not repay the mortgage, the lender can pursue you for any remaining debt.

The mortgage default rate has traditionally been low—typically around 0.2%—making mortgages an attractive business for lenders, who have benefited from Japan's modest levels of unemployment and divorce, two common default triggers. In the fall of 2009, however, the default rate began to increase as the effects of the recession spread throughout the economy.

The approval process
It can take 30–60 days to arrange a mortgage, with some lenders differentiating their services by offering rapid approvals. There are three steps in the process, although it is possible to skip the first two and go right to a full application:

1. **Indicative approval.** You complete an application form, but you don't provide any supporting documents about yourself or the home you wish to buy. Based on this information, the lender indicates how much it is willing to lend and at what rate. This is a nonbinding estimate and is subject to the lender verifying your information, receiving supporting documents and approving the property. Obtaining an indicative approval can help you establish a realistic budget for your home purchase. Indicative approval is only available from foreign lenders.

2. **Preapproval.** You complete an application form and provide supporting documents about your job, residency and finances. The lender indicates how much it is willing to lend and at what rate. The estimate is still not binding, but you can begin shopping for a home with more confidence that the mortgage will be approved.

3. **Full approval.** You complete an application form and provide supporting documents about yourself and the home you want to buy and copies of the sale and purchase agreement and explanation of important matters. After reviewing the documents, the lender makes a binding offer that you can accept or reject.

Mortgage applications are refused for many reasons, including the borrower carrying too much debt or being ill, too old or unable to document his income. These issues can and should be addressed with your lender before you go shopping.

Property-specific issues can also cause the lender to reject a mortgage application. These include a home outside the lender's geographical or policy limits, such as a ski chalet in Hokkaido; missing documents, such as a certificate of post construction (*kensa zumisho*); a large gap between the purchase price and the appraised value; and new zoning regulations that require a condominium to have fewer units if it is redeveloped. Some lenders will tell you that the mortgage application has been approved but the property has been rejected and suggest that you find another. Others will simply reject your application outright.

Your ability to obtain a mortgage will also be influenced by branch-level sales quotas, changes to a lender's credit rating and underwriting guidelines, the Bank of Japan's policy decisions and global events, such as the failure of Lehman Brothers.

If you have the money, paying cash can be an effective strategy because it lets you close the transaction quickly without waiting for a mortgage approval. You can then refinance the property, but you must have all of the documentation that you would have gathered to obtain a mortgage. Without a full set of documents, you may be unable to arrange refinancing.

Obtaining a mortgage

To arrange a mortgage, you can approach a lender directly or through an intermediary.

The direct approach works best with foreign banks operating in Japan, such as Commonwealth Bank of Australia (www.commbank. co.jp), The Hongkong and Shanghai Banking Corp. (www.hsbc.co.jp) or National Australia Bank (www.nabasia.co.jp). It is also effective if you have a private banking relationship or are arranging a mortgage offshore with a bank that is not licensed to operate in Japan. Offshore mortgages are typically secured with assets such as real estate in another country.

The indirect approach, which involves a paid or unpaid introduction, is appropriate for domestic lenders. Real estate agents and developers who have a business relationship with one or more lenders are a common source of introductions. The agent or developer will be familiar with the lenders' policies and will have a personal relationship with loan officers that facilitates informal communication. That relationship won't guarantee success, but it will ensure your application is presented in the right format and with the correct documents.

Agents and developers don't charge for an introduction. Instead, they use their ability to introduce you to lenders as a marketing tool. One potential drawback to this approach is that the lenders with which the agent or developer has a relationship may not offer the best deal. Fortunately, the mortgage business is competitive and you can check the rate against those posted on www.eloan.co.jp (Japanese only), which aggregates information from more than 60 lenders.

Mortgage brokers such as IFG Asia Mortgages (www.ifgasiamortgages.com) are another way to find funding. Unlike agents and developers who work with one or two lenders, brokers know many financial institutions. Brokers use this knowledge to match your circumstances (funding requirements; age; immigration, employment and marital status; assets; income and credit history) with the lender that is most likely to accept your application and offer a competitive financing package. The broker can tailor your application to the lender, ensuring that you have all the necessary paperwork and that it is presented correctly.

Brokers charge the borrower a fee for their services. For example, IFG provides a free initial consultation, where they explain their services and prescreen the borrower to ensure the loan application has a reasonable chance of success. If the application is viable and the borrower wants to proceed, she supplies her personal details, indicates the amount she wants to borrow and pays a nonrefundable application fee. IFG then submits mortgage applications to several lenders. If the application is successful, IFG charges the borrower a percentage of the mortgage amount. There is a minimum charge and, aside from the initial application fee, borrowers only pay IFG when their mortgage is drawn down. IFG can arrange refinancing as well as mortgages for residential, commercial and investment properties and vacant land.

Brokers add the most value when they arrange a mortgage from a large Japanese bank, because these banks offer the best rates but are least likely to lend to a non-Japanese borrower. Brokers can also be helpful if your situation is complicated or unusual, or you lack the time or inclination to search for a lender. Ask the broker for client references and examples of mortgages he has arranged from different lenders to gauge the breadth of his contacts.

Keep it simple

In 2007, Susan Woodward analyzed the closing costs and terms of 7,560 30-year fixed-rate mortgages that were made throughout the United States and guaranteed by the U.S. Federal Housing Administration.[1]

Woodward found that mortgages arranged by brokers cost borrowers about $600 more than those obtained through direct lenders. She also found that sources of complexity, such as points (fees paid to a lender to induce them to make a loan) and seller contributions to closing costs, made mortgages more expensive. Borrowers who used "no-cost" loans that allowed them to shop on the basis of interest rates alone paid $1,200 less than borrowers who paid some lender or broker fees in cash.

While Woodward's research focused on the U.S., dealing directly with a lender and favoring simple mortgage products over complex ones will save you money in any market.

Choosing a lender

Your choice of lender will be determined by your residency status, language ability and credit history. A Japanese-speaking permanent resident (PR) who is employed by a well-known Japanese company and has an established credit record can take advantage of large local banks' lower interest rates. A less fluent resident who doesn't have PR status will probably have more success with a midsized bank, while a Japan- or Hong Kong–based buyer who doesn't speak Japanese will get a more sympathetic hearing from an international bank. Someone buying property outside Japan's large cities may find that a smaller local bank is helpful.

As a rule, the lowest interest rates come with the least flexibility and English-language service. The reverse is also true. The more accommodating the lender and the more English spoken, the higher the rates. The Japanese mortgage market is competitive, however, so shop around. International banks like National Australia Bank (NAB) and Commonwealth Bank of Australia (CBA) can be a competitive source of funding for investment properties.

You should also consider whether you want the lender to provide day-to-day banking services. For example, Bank of Tokyo-Mitsubishi UFJ (www.bk.mufg.jp) has nearly 800 branches, Sumitomo Mitsui Banking Corp. (www.smbc.co.jp) has over 600, Suruga Bank (www.surugabank.co.jp) has more than 110, Shinsei Bank (www.shinseibank.com) has fewer than 40, The Hongkong and Shanghai Banking Corp. (HSBC) has seven, NAB has two and CBA has one.

The Australian banks offer a limited range of services and no automated teller machines (ATMs) in Japan, while the other lenders offer a full range of retail banking services. Shinsei Bank and HSBC have relatively small ATM networks that are supplemented by partnership agreements with other operators. Mizuho Bank (www.mizuhobank.co.jp), by comparison, operates more than 5,500 ATMs nationwide.

Large Japanese banks

Large Japanese banks—such as the Bank of Tokyo-Mitsubishi UFJ, Chuo Mitsui Trust and Banking Co. (www.chuomitsui.jp), Mitsubishi UFJ Trust and Banking Corp. (www.tr.mufg.jp), Mizuho Bank, Mizuho Trust Bank (www.mizuho-tb.co.jp), Resona Bank (www.resona-gr.co.jp/resonabank, Japanese only), Sumitomo Mitsui Banking Corp. and Sumitomo Trust & Banking Co. (www.sumitomotrust.co.jp)— offer the lowest mortgage rates.

Fixed-rate, hybrid and variable-rate mortgages are available from these banks for the purchase of new and used residential property (i.e., detached houses and condominiums), construction of new homes, refinancing, repairs and improvements such as making homes barrier-free. Equity release mortgages are available and many banks offer lower interest rates for energy-efficient and low-CO_2 homes and for houses using solar energy. Banks also offer mortgages that include health insurance riders, a repayment holiday in the event of a natural disaster and revolving credit lines.

Large Japanese banks usually require borrowers to join a group life insurance plan. Banks charge a guarantee fee of about 2% of the mortgage amount, which is usually paid to a subsidiary or affiliated company. This differs from the mortgage insurance available in other countries that is provided by an independent third party. The guarantee fee varies from bank to bank and you can usually pay a slightly higher interest rate for the duration of the mortgage instead of the guarantee fee. This can reduce your initial outlay, but will cost you more over the life of a 35-year mortgage.

Flat 35 and Flat 50

From 1950 to 2003, the Government Housing Loan Corporation (GHLC) provided mortgages directly to individuals and was the main lender for the government's housing policies. In 2007, the GHLC was succeeded by the Japan Housing Finance Agency (JHF), which withdrew from the direct lending business. The JHF now purchases and securitizes mortgages originated by private lenders, underwrites mortgage insurance and provides loans for urban redevelopment projects and the construction of rental housing for the elderly and families with small children.

Flat 35 (www.flat35.com, Japanese only) is a long-term, fixed-interest mortgage offered by banks and other lenders in collaboration with the JHF, which buys claims on the mortgages from lenders and then issues securities using the mortgages as collateral. When the borrower draws down the mortgage, the lender sells its claim against the mortgage to the JHF. However, the interest rate, repayment schedule and other terms and conditions remain unchanged and the borrower makes payments to the lender from which he obtained the mortgage. There is no penalty for early repayment of a Flat 35 mortgage.

The interest rate for Flat 35 mortgages varies among lenders because the interest rate comprises three components: the coupon rate of the mortgage-backed security issued by the JHF; the JHF's operational cost; and a service fee, which is set by the financial institution that originates the mortgage.[2] In addition, some lenders have introduced complexities, such as loan fees and interest rates that change over the course of the mortgage term, making it difficult to compare offers from different financial institutions.

In April 2009, Flat 35 was modified under the government's economic stimulus plan. The maximum loan amount was increased from 90% to 100% of a home's construction cost or purchase price, a 0.3% interest rate reduction was extended from 10 to 20 years for certain types of property, refinancing loans were introduced and home buyers could borrow to pay for inspection fees and other miscellaneous expenses. In December 2009, the interest rate cut was increased again, from 0.3% to 1.0%.

The JHF also offers Flat 50 (www.flat35.com/kaitei/flat50_start.html, Japanese only), a 50-year, fixed-rate mortgage that includes a "relay" feature allowing the child of a borrower to take over the mortgage. Flat 35 and Flat 50 mortgages are available to qualified permanent residents.

To obtain a mortgage from a top-tier Japanese bank, it helps to understand the bank's perspective on you and your application. First, as a non-Japanese borrower, you are not a mainstream client. Banks haven't designed products to meet your requirements, as they have with temporary workers or single women, and their systems are not built to accommodate your needs.

Unless you have lived in Japan for an extended period, you will not have a local credit record (see below). This makes it difficult for banks to evaluate your creditworthiness, particularly given that your credit history outside Japan is usually seen as irrelevant. Lenders focus on income rather than assets when evaluating your ability to repay a mortgage, which is a rational policy given the declines in Japanese stock and land prices over the past two decades. Lenders also prefer borrowers with little or no outstanding debt.

Even if you read and write Japanese fluently, there will be questions about your ability to comprehend the terms of the loan agreement and other documents, all of which will be in Japanese.

The bank may be concerned that, as a foreigner, you will not be aware of, or observe, the conventions that keep Japanese society running smoothly. They may be afraid that you'll demand special treatment, write outraged letters to the *Japan Times,* sue the bank or flee the country.

Traditionally, Japanese lenders have relied on "soft" information rather than the credit scoring formulas used in other countries.[3] This approach gives the loan officer and branch staff more flexibility in approving or rejecting your mortgage application. As Jason Foutch of Century 21 Smica Create observes, "If I apply for a loan through the Roppongi branch and I apply for a loan through the Naka-Meguro branch, one will go through and one won't, even if it's the same bank with the same documentation. It's all down to the loan officer."

Your mortgage application must be letter-perfect and internally consistent. Minor variations in spelling or capitalization that a native English speaker would ignore can cause your application to be delayed or rejected. You may also be required to produce originals or notarized copies of documents, which can be time-consuming.

Despite these challenges, many foreign residents have obtained mortgages from Japan's large banks. Here's how to increase the likelihood that your application will be approved:

- **Become a permanent resident.** Meeting the government's PR requirements tells the bank you are a person of good character and are creditworthy. It also suggests you have strong ties to Japan and are unlikely to flee.

- **Speak and read Japanese.** Fluency in Japanese makes it easier for the bank to serve you. It also helps to allay concerns about you understanding and complying with the mortgage agreement.

- **Demonstrate ties to the community.** Having a Japanese spouse, having children living in Japan and applying for PR (even if it has not yet been approved) demonstrate that you are in Japan for the long term and are a good risk.

- **Exude stability.** Banks like borrowers who have worked for the same employer (ideally a large, well-known Japanese company) for a long time. Having three jobs in as many years, even with increases in salary and responsibility, does not work in your favor. Entertainers and entrepreneurs are seen as poor risks because their incomes are more volatile than those of salaried employees.

- **Have your paperwork in order.** You will save time and make it easier for the bank to approve your application if you have all of the documents (see below) the lender needs in their preferred format.

- **Be conventional.** You are more likely to get a mortgage for a Tokyo condominium than an organic farm in Hokkaido. For face-to-face appointments, dress appropriately.

- **Use introductions.** A referral from your real estate agent, developer, employer, spouse's family or even a politician can open doors that would otherwise remain shut.

- **Make the numbers work.** Ensure your loan-to-value ratio (mortgage amount divided by the property's value), debt-to-income ratio (annual mortgage repayment divided by your annual income), mortgage amount and term are within the ranges specified by the bank. The larger your down payment, the less risk the lender perceives.

- **Leave some wiggle room.** Add 7%–8% to the purchase price for closing costs and incidentals and budget for repairs and maintenance. Buying a little less than you can afford is sensible, especially in an era of deflation, salary and bonus cuts and layoffs.

Credit bureaus

Japan has three national consumer credit bureaus: the Personal Credit Information Center, the Credit Information Center and the Japan Credit Information Reference Center.

Unlike in Canada and the United States, where positive and negative information from many sources is aggregated by competing credit bureaus, Japan's credit reporting is fragmented. Not all members share all their data and often only negative information, such as late payments, is retained. In addition, the credit bureaus do not use a standardized scoring framework.[4]

Operated by the Japanese Bankers Association (www.zenginkyo.or.jp), the Personal Credit Information Center represents banks, other financial institutions, bank-affiliated credit card issuers and guarantee companies. The Personal Credit Information Center collects information about consumer loans, current account transactions, guarantees and credit card transactions. The Japanese section of the association's site explains how to check your credit file by mail or in person at the association's offices in Fukuoka, Hiroshima, Kobe, Kyoto, Nagoya, Osaka, Sapporo, Sendai, Tokyo and Yokohama.

Members of the Credit Information Center (www.cic.co.jp) include department stores, as well as credit card, finance, consumer credit, leasing, insurance and credit guarantee companies. The center tracks credit card transactions, installment credit sales, leasing contracts, guarantees, loans and mortgages. It also operates the Credit Information Network, the system through which Japan's credit bureaus share consumers' credit information. You can check your credit record by mail or in person at the center's offices in Fukuoka, Hiroshima, Kanazawa, Nagoya, Osaka, Sapporo, Sendai, Takamatsu and Tokyo.

Formerly known as the Japan Information Center, the Japan Credit Information Reference Center (www.jicc.co.jp) represents credit card, consumer credit and finance companies. You can check your credit record by mail or in person at the center's offices in Osaka and Tokyo.

For more information on credit ratings and consumer lending, see the Japan Consumer Credit Industry Association (www.j-credit.or.jp, Japanese only).

Midsized Japanese banks

Two midsized banks, Shinsei Bank and Suruga Bank, offer mortgages to permanent residents. Both banks have English-language Websites and marketing materials.

Shinsei offers fixed- and variable-rate mortgages for the purchase of new or used residential property and refinancing. Mortgage amounts range from ¥5 million to ¥100 million with terms of 5–35 years. Shinsei does not charge a guarantor fee or an early repayment fee and operates an English-speaking call center and bilingual ATMs and online banking services. Shinsei will lend to nonpermanent residents who are married to Japanese citizens or permanent residents. Borrowers must join a group life insurance plan selected by Shinsei and pay a ¥50,000 handling fee if the mortgage is approved. Borrowers must be over age 20 and under 65 when the loan is originated and under 80 when the last payment is due.

Suruga provides mortgages for the purchase of residential property or land for personal use, home improvements and refinancing. Mortgages are variable rate, with amounts of ¥1 million to ¥100 million and terms of 1–35 years. A guarantor is not necessary, but the borrower must join a group life insurance plan selected by Suruga. A sliding scale of prepayment charges applies for the life of the loan and Suruga charges a ¥105,000 handling fee if the mortgage is approved. Suruga has marketing materials in Portuguese, Spanish, Korean and Chinese, but requires that borrowers have some competence in Japanese. Borrowers must be over age 20 and under 65 when the loan is originated and under 76 when the last payment is due.

In addition to their small branch and ATM networks, the main disadvantage to dealing with these banks is that their interest rates can be higher than those of large Japanese banks.

Foreign banks

Three foreign-domiciled banks—Commonwealth Bank of Australia, The Hongkong and Shanghai Banking Corp. and National Australia Bank—are licensed to operate in Japan and offer mortgages that use Japanese residential property as security. These banks prefer to lend against property in major cities, such as Tokyo, Yokohama, Osaka and Nagoya, because these markets are liquid and it is easier to obtain accurate valuations. CBA and NAB offered mortgages for recreational property in Niseko but have discontinued this service. HSBC provides mortgages throughout Japan.

The three banks provide English-language Websites and marketing materials and English-speaking staff. Unlike their local counterparts, CBA, HSBC and NAB consider your financial history and assets outside Japan and use Western-style credit scoring systems that are more foreigner-friendly. The international banks will also lend for investment properties and equity release, which domestic banks sometimes avoid. These advantages are offset by higher interest rates, smaller branch networks and CBA and NAB's limited product offerings.

Commonwealth Bank of Australia provides mortgages for new or used residential property, off-the-plan purchases, refinancing and equity release. Borrowers must be over age 20, but do not have to be permanent residents or reside in Japan. Nonresidents must live in a country or territory where CBA has a branch. CBA lends to individuals as well as companies.

CBA's mortgages can be denominated in yen; Australian, New Zealand, United States, Singapore or Hong Kong dollars; British pounds; or euros. Yen-denominated mortgages can have a maximum loan-to-value (LTV) ratio of 80%, while non-yen mortgages are limited to 75%. The maximum LTV ratio is 80% for urban properties and 50% for nonurban properties. Mortgages are variable rate, based on CBA's cost of funds plus 2% per annum, with a minimum size of ¥15 million and a term of 3–25 years. There is a sliding scale of prepayment fees, ranging from ¥300,000 to ¥500,000, and an application fee of ¥210,000 is payable when the mortgage is funded.

HSBC's mortgages are only available to customers who have opened a Premier account, which requires a minimum balance of ¥10 million, or its foreign currency equivalent, on deposit with HSBC in Japan. HSBC will lend for refinancing, the purchase of new or used residential property (including investment property) and the construction of a new house.

HSBC has two mortgage products. Both have a minimum loan amount of ¥10 million and do not require a guarantor or life insurance. The minimum prepayment is ¥1 million, which is subject to a 1.05% fee, and English-language translations of the loan documents are available for ¥105,000. Borrowers must be over age 20 and under 60 when the loan is originated and under 80 when the last payment is due.

HSBC Smart Mortgage is available to Japanese nationals, permanent residents and foreigners with a Japanese spouse and offers a term of 1–35 years and a maximum LTV ratio of 90%. A handling fee of ¥73,500 is charged if the mortgage is approved.

Permanent residency is not required for HSBC Smart Investment Mortgage, which offers a term of 1–25 years and a maximum LTV ratio of 70%. This mortgage cannot be used to buy commercial property, and a handling fee of ¥105,000 is payable if the mortgage is approved.

Two interest rate options are available for HSBC Smart Mortgage and HSBC Smart Investment Mortgage. The first option uses a fixed or variable base rate to which a second interest charge is added if the LTV ratio exceeds 60% or 80%. The second option deducts the balance of the borrower's bank account from the outstanding mortgage amount for interest-calculation purposes.

National Australia Bank offers mortgages to buy new or used residential property in Tokyo, Chiba, Kanagawa, Saitama, Kobe, Kyoto and Osaka. NAB will also lend for off-the-plan purchases, refinancing and equity release. Borrowers must be residents of Japan (permanent residency is not mandatory), Australia, Hong Kong or Singapore. Individuals, companies and trusts are eligible. Owner-occupiers must be under age 75 and people buying investment property must be under 65 at the end of the mortgage.

NAB's mortgages are denominated in yen, with a maximum term of 20 years for nonresident investors, 25 years for resident investors and 35 years for owner-occupiers. The minimum loan amount is ¥10 million and there is no charge for prepayment. Variable-rate mortgages are based on NAB's cost of funds plus 2% per annum for amounts over ¥30 million or cost plus 2.5% for amounts under ¥30 million. Five-year, fixed-rate mortgages may be available. NAB charges an establishment fee of 0.6% of the mortgage value, which is payable when the mortgage is approved.

The Herman case

No overview of financing a property purchase in Japan would be complete without mentioning Steven L. Herman, an American journalist who lived in Japan from 1990 to 2007.

In June 1999, Steve signed a contract to purchase a ¥75 million condominium in Shibuya, in central Tokyo. Steve—who had been dealing with Asahi Bank (now part of the Resona Group) in a personal and corporate capacity for several years—applied to Asahi Bank for a ¥68.5 million mortgage for his new home.

At the time, Steve was a senior executive at a multinational media organization and was earning a salary he describes as several times that of a typical Japanese manager. He had a solid credit history, had lived in Japan for nearly a decade and spoke Japanese, but was not a permanent resident.

Despite his credentials, he was unsuccessful. "I wasn't turned down for a mortgage," observes Steve. "They refused to accept the application."

Steve says that when his then-fiancé met Asahi Bank representatives to ask why they wouldn't consider his application, they told her it was because, "Foreigners run away."

As Steve explains, "If I had filed an application and they turned me down and said, 'No, we've reviewed your application and we don't want to give you a loan,' then that's their right. I thought they were extremely insensitive and were being blatantly discriminatory and that's why I decided to file the suit."

In October 1999, Steve sued Asahi Bank in Tokyo District Court seeking ¥11 million in damages. His attorney argued that Asahi Bank's lending practices were discriminatory, unconstitutional and violated Steve's human rights under international law.

Asahi Bank claimed it was against their policy to provide loans to foreigners without permanent resident status because they would not be able to recover the outstanding money if the borrower fled overseas.

In November 2001, the Tokyo District Court ruled in favor of Asahi Bank. Steve filed an appeal with the Tokyo High Court, which was dismissed in August 2002. He then appealed to Japan's Supreme Court, which declined to hear the case. The case was subsequently cited in a United Nations report on the prevention of discrimination against noncitizens.[5]

Steve believes the effort was worthwhile. "Even though we lost at every level from a legal point of view, we did apparently change the mindset of banks in Japan," says Steve, who later became a permanent resident and purchased a home in Tokyo's Ota-ku with a loan from Fuji Bank (now Mizuho Bank).

And despite spending "many, many thousands of dollars," he believes it was a Pyrrhic victory for Asahi Bank. "This must have cost them an enormous amount of money. In fact, I'm sure the legal case from their side cost them more money than if I had taken a loan and defaulted on it."

Supporting documents

Here are the documents a lender is likely to request to support your mortgage application. Different documents will be required depending on the lender, type of property, whether you are an owner-occupier or investor and your country of residence. You are unlikely to need everything on this list, but some lenders may request additional items. Original documents or notarized copies may be required, and some documents have expiry dates.

You will also need to complete a mortgage application form and a consent form that allows the lender to check your references. The consent form may also authorize the lender to retrieve official documents on your behalf. There will also be a life insurance application, if you are joining a group plan through the lender.

Identification

- Valid passport with valid visa, and/or valid driver's license for you and your spouse, if applicable.

- Alien registration card (*gaikokujin toroku shomeisho*; 外国人登録証明書) and/or certificate of alien registration (*gaikokujin toroku genpyo kisai jikou shomeisho*; 外国人登録原票記載事項証明書) for you and your spouse, if applicable.

- Resident's registration certificate (*jumin hyo*; 住民票), which is needed if you or your spouse is a Japanese national or if your Japanese spouse will act as guarantor. The certificate should include all family members in the household registered to that address and the loan applicant's relation to the guarantor. The certificate is valid for three months from the date of issue and is available from the ward or city office.

- Registered seal (*jitsu-in*; 実印). This is purchased from a stamp (*hanko*) shop and registered with your local ward office.

- Three certified copies of your seal (*inkan toroku shomeisho*; 印鑑登録証明書). Available from the ward or city office where your seal is registered, these are valid for three months from the date of issue.

- Valid national health insurance card (*kenko hoken sho*; 健康保険証).

- Name, address, phone and fax numbers and email address of your real estate agent and judicial scrivener (*shiho-shoshi*; 司法書士).

Financial

- Pay slips or bank statements showing three months of salary history. An employment report may be needed if you have been with your employer for less than three years.

- Employment contract (*koyou keiyakusho*; 雇用契約書). This is usually needed if you have been with your employer for less than one year.

- Statement of withholding tax paid for the past two years (*gensen choshuhyo*; 源泉徴収票). Available from your employer.

- Inhabitants tax certificate (*juminzei kazei shomeisho*; 住民税課税証明書) or inhabitants tax notice (*juminzei kettei tsuchisho*; 住民税決定通知書). Available from your ward or city office.

- Special income tax return (*kakutei shinkokusho hikae*; 確定申告書控え). People who are self-employed or have multiple income sources or income over ¥20 million must file this document with the regional tax office each year.

- Tax payment certificate (*nozei shomeisho*; 納税証明書その１、その２). Available from your ward or city office, this includes a set of two documents for the past two years and is needed if you filed your own income tax return (*kakutei shinkoku*; 確定申告).

- Schedule of repayments and outstanding balance for other mortgaged property you own.

- Account statements for other debts, such as credit cards or car loans.

- Proof of ownership of other assets, such as stocks, bonds, property or bank accounts is required by some foreign lenders.

- If you are self-employed or using a company to apply for the mortgage, you will need the company registration (*tokibo tohon*; 登記簿謄本) and two or three years of financial statements (*kessansho*; 決算書) and tax returns.

Property

- Sale and purchase agreement (*baibai keiyakusho*; 売買契約書). Available from the real estate agent.

- Construction contract (*ukeoi keiyakusho*; 請負契約書) or cost estimate (*oyobi mitsumorisho*; 及び見積もり書). Available from the vendor, developer or builder.

- Explanation of important matters (*juyou jikou setsumeisho*; 重要事項説明書). This is available from the real estate agent, who reads it aloud before the contract is signed.

- Certificate of post construction (*kensa zumisho*; 検査済証 ［建物］). Available from the vendor, developer or builder.

- Building permit (*kakunin zumisho;* 確認済証 ［建物］). Available from the vendor, developer or builder.

- Building plan layout (*tatemono haichizu;* 建物配置図). Available from the vendor, developer or builder.

- Land registration certificate (*tokijikou shomeisho [tokibo tohon];* 登記事項証明書 ［土地］). Available from the Legal Affairs Bureau (*houmukyoku;* 法務局).

- Building registration certificate (*tokijikou shomeisho [tokibo tohon];* 登記事項証明書 ［建物］). Available from the Legal Affairs Bureau.

- Official land map (*kouzu;* 公図). Available from the Legal Affairs Bureau.

- Property brochure (*bukken gaiyo [hanbai zumen];* 物件概要 ［販売図面］). Available from the real estate agent or developer.

- Statement of income and expenses (*shushi meisai;* 物件収支明細). Available from the vendor or management company.

- Property location map (*bukken annaizu;* 物件案内図). Needed for new condominiums and houses, this is available from the real estate agent.

- Acreage survey map (*chiseki sokuryouzu;* 地積測量図). Available from the Legal Affairs Bureau.

- Building floor plan (*tatemono heimenzu;* 建物平面図). Available from the builder or the Legal Affairs Bureau.

- Building inspection certificate (*tatemono kensazumisho;* 建物検査済証). Needed for new condominiums and houses, this is available from the builder or real estate agent.

- Original title deed (*kenrisho;* 権利書原本). Available from the vendor after the title is transferred.

Insurance

- Proof of fire insurance, including the insurer's name, policy number and insured amount.

- Proof of earthquake insurance, including the insurer's name, policy number and insured amount.

- Proof of life insurance, including the insurer's name, policy number and insured amount, if the insurance is not provided by the lender.

INSURANCE

Life insurance

Many lenders will not approve a mortgage unless you enroll in a group life insurance plan. The lender usually specifies the insurer, pays the premium and is named as the policy's beneficiary.

If you have had a major health problem, such as cancer or a heart attack, within the past three years, you are unlikely to qualify for life insurance. Chronic conditions such as diabetes mellitus, hypertension, cirrhosis or renal disease will also cause you to be disqualified. Shopping around is pointless because different insurers use the same terms. Your insurance coverage can be revoked if you are discovered to have omitted information on your application.

Fire insurance

Lenders require fire insurance for the duration of the mortgage.

Earthquake insurance

Despite Japan's reputation as a seismic hotspot, earthquake insurance for residential dwellings is readily available. In fiscal 2007, Japanese households had over ¥91 trillion in earthquake coverage and 44% of fire insurance policies included an earthquake rider.

Reinsurance

Under the Law Concerning Earthquake Insurance (Law No. 73, 1966), coverage is provided by non-life insurance companies, which are reinsured by the Japan Earthquake Reinsurance Company (JER). JER, in turn, has retrocession agreements, under which JER is reinsured by the non-life insurance companies and the Japanese government.

There is an aggregate liability limit of ¥5.5 trillion for any one earthquake with the contribution of JER, the non-life insurance companies and the government varying according to the amount of claims payable.[1] If total losses exceed ¥5.5 trillion, insurance companies can reduce their payouts to policy holders. To put the liability cap in perspective, claims worth ¥78.3 billion were paid after the Great Hanshin Earthquake in 1995.

Buying earthquake insurance

Earthquake insurance is sold as a rider to fire insurance policies and is not available separately. Fire insurance does not cover losses from fires caused or spread by an earthquake. You can add earthquake coverage to a valid fire insurance policy, but you may not be able to do so if an earthquake warning is in effect. Earthquake insurance is available in terms of one to five years.

Condominiums built with steel-reinforced concrete have excellent earthquake resistance.

Coverage

Earthquake insurance covers loss or damage to residential buildings and personal property through fire, destruction, burial or flooding caused directly or indirectly by an earthquake, volcanic eruption or tsunami. Loss or damage is excluded if it is caused by gross negligence, willful or illegal acts, war or insurrection, or if it occurs 10 or more days after an earthquake.

The sum insured ranges from 30% to 50% of the amount of the fire insurance policy to which the earthquake rider is attached. Coverage is limited to ¥50 million for a building and ¥10 million for personal property. Losses are categorized as total, half or partial, and the amount payable is based on the depreciated value of the insured property.

Premiums

Earthquake insurance premiums are standardized and based on the dwelling's location and whether it is constructed from wood. Wooden structures cost more to insure and Tokyo, Kanagawa and Shizuoka are the most expensive locations.

Discounts are available for long-term contracts, buildings constructed after 1981 and buildings that have been assessed as earthquake-resistant or seismically isolated. Discounts are also offered for buildings that are rated as earthquake-resistant on the Housing Quality Assurance Act's three-point scale. Earthquake insurance premiums can be deducted from income and local inhabitants taxes.

By way of illustration, ¥20 million of earthquake insurance on a wooden dwelling in Tokyo built in 2001 would cost ¥56,340 per year. Note that this amount excludes the cost of the basic fire insurance and earthquake coverage for personal property.

TAX

Individuals and companies that buy, own, sell or earn rental income from property in Japan are subject to Japanese taxes.* The tax obligation will depend on whether the property is owner-occupied or held as an investment; the owner's residency status; the length of time the property is held; and whether the property is acquired by an individual or a company. Consumption tax is payable on buildings and most of the services associated with buying and selling property. Exemptions and allowances are available for many of these taxes, which are levied by national, prefectural and municipal governments.

Background

Appraised values

Taxes on acquiring and holding property are based on government-sponsored appraisals. The appraised value often bears little relationship to a property's market price.

The posted price is based on a nationwide appraisal of 30,000 parcels of land by the Ministry of Land, Infrastructure, Transport and Tourism. Prices are effective January 1 and are announced in late March each year.

The standard price is derived from a nationwide appraisal of more than 24,000 sites that is commissioned by municipal governments. Prices are effective July 1 and are announced in late September each year.

The roadside price is an appraisal of major urban roads that is commissioned by the National Tax Agency. Prices are assigned to the road (not the adjacent property) and are used to calculate the value

*This is an overview, not a substitute for professional advice. It is intended for individuals, not corporate investors.

of properties for inheritance and gift taxes. Roadside prices are typically about 80% of the posted price. The roadside price is effective January 1 and is announced in August each year.

The fixed property valuation is conducted at 450,000 sites every three years. It is effective January 1 and used to calculate the registration license tax, fixed asset tax and real estate acquisition tax. The fixed property valuation is approximately 70% of the posted price.[1]

Residency

In Japan, the way in which your income is taxed depends on whether you are a nonresident, a permanent resident or a nonpermanent resident.[2] These categories reflect your tax status, not your status with the Immigration Bureau.

For tax purposes, you automatically become a permanent resident when you have lived in Japan for five years (60 months) in the previous 10 years. Permanent residents are taxed on their worldwide income and are subject to national income tax and local taxes.

Nonpermanent residents do not intend to live permanently in Japan. They have resided in Japan for more than one year but less than five years in the past 10 years. Nonpermanent residents are subject to Japanese tax on income earned in Japan and on income earned offshore and remitted into Japan.

Nonresidents do not intend to reside permanently in Japan and have lived in Japan for less than one year. They are generally subject to withholding tax on rental income earned in Japan and capital gains taxes on the sale of property in Japan.[3] Nonresident investors are not subject to local taxes.

Income earned in Japan may be subject to special measures that prevent double taxation if you are a citizen of Armenia, Australia, Austria, Azerbaijan, Bangladesh, Belarus, Belgium, Brazil, Bulgaria, Canada, China,* the Czech Republic, Denmark, Fiji, Finland, France, Georgia, Germany, Egypt, Hungary, India, Indonesia, Ireland, Israel, Italy, Kyrgyzstan, Luxembourg, Malaysia, Mexico, Moldova, the Netherlands, New Zealand, Norway, Pakistan, the Philippines, Poland, Romania, Russia, Singapore, Slovakia, South Africa, South Korea, Spain, Sri Lanka, Sweden, Switzerland, Tajikistan, Thailand, Turkey, Turkmenistan, Ukraine, the United Kingdom, the United States, Uzbekistan, Vietnam or Zambia.[4]

*Japan's tax treaty with China does not include the Hong Kong and Macau special administrative regions.

Double taxation agreements do not usually offer relief from withholding tax on rental income or capital gains tax from the sale of property in Japan. But, for example, a resident of Australia can generally avoid double taxation by claiming a tax credit in Australia for taxes paid on rental income or capital gains in Japan. For more information, see a tax expert in your home country.

Where to pay

Taxes can be paid at the tax office, the post office and at financial institutions such as banks. You can also pay taxes using a mobile phone or personal computer, although this service must be arranged with your bank.

In Tokyo, the real estate acquisition tax, fixed asset tax and urban planning tax can be paid at convenience stores and at designated automated teller machines.[5]

Stamps used to pay stamp tax (see below) can be purchased from the post office. Stamp tax can also be paid in cash at the tax office.[6]

The National Tax Agency will not accept payments from offshore bank accounts.

Acquisition taxes

Consumption tax

A 5% consumption tax is payable on buildings, construction contracts, real estate agents' commissions and most of the services associated with buying and selling property. Comprising a 4% national tax and a 1% local tax, consumption tax is not payable on the sale of land, on residential rents or on mortgages.[7]

Real estate acquisition tax

Buyers of residential property are subject to a one-time acquisition tax of 1.5% of the value of the land and 3.0% of the value of the building, based on the fixed property valuation. This prefectural tax is due within a few months of your purchase and does not apply to inherited property. The judicial scrivener notifies the tax office of your purchase within a period set by the prefecture.

The tax rates for nonresidential land and buildings are 3.0% and 4.0%, respectively. From April 1, 2012, the rate will be 4.0% for residential and nonresidential land and buildings.

Registration and license tax

Based on the fixed property valuation, this national tax is paid on the transfer or retention of property. Until March 31, 2011, the rate for the transfer of ownership by sale is 1.0% of the value of the building and 2.0% of the value of the land. The rate for buildings will increase to 1.3%, 1.5% and 2.0% at the start of fiscal 2011, 2012 and 2013, respectively. The rate for land will remain at 2.0%.

Registration and license tax is also payable on mortgages at a rate of 0.4% of the loan amount.

Stamp tax

This national tax is levied on contracts, including those for mortgages, leases, construction and the sale of property. Stamp tax is based on the contract amount and is paid by the buyer or borrower.

Stamp tax rates			
	Contract type		
Value	Construction	Property purchase	Lease or mortgage
Less than ¥10,000	¥0	¥0	¥0
¥100,000 and below	¥200	¥200	¥200
¥500,000 and below	¥200	¥400	¥400
¥1 million and below	¥200	¥1,000	¥1,000
¥2 million and below	¥400	¥2,000	¥2,000
¥3 million and below	¥1,000	¥2,000	¥2,000
¥5 million and below	¥2,000	¥2,000	¥2,000
¥10 million and below	¥10,000	¥10,000	¥10,000
¥50 million and below	¥15,000	¥15,000	¥20,000
¥100 million and below	¥45,000	¥45,000	¥60,000
¥500 million and below	¥80,000	¥80,000	¥100,000
¥1 billion and below	¥180,000	¥180,000	¥200,000
¥5 billion and below	¥360,000	¥360,000	¥400,000
More than ¥5 billion	¥540,000	¥540,000	¥600,000

Ownership taxes

Fixed property tax

This municipal tax is based on the fixed property valuation. The standard rate is 1.4% of the value of the building and land, but there are numerous adjustments and deductions.

The fixed property tax is generally payable in four installments each year. Owners of property in the tax register on January 1 must pay this tax for the fiscal year beginning April 1, even if the property is sold on January 2.

In Tokyo and other jurisdictions, you must inform the tax office if you buy, enlarge, demolish or rebuild a house; convert a house to a non-residential use or vice versa; or change the use of vacant land. The tax office must also be notified if a house is destroyed in a natural disaster.

Urban planning tax

This municipal tax is capped at 0.3% of the fixed property valuation. Urban planning tax is collected with the fixed property tax and is payable in quarterly installments.

The urban planning tax is generally higher in large cities. In Tokyo, the fixed property tax and urban planning tax are collected as a prefectural tax.

Income and disposal taxes

Capital gains

For individual investors who are residents of Japan, gains on the sale of real estate that has been held for less than five years are taxed at a minimum rate of 39%: a 30% national tax plus a 9% local inhabitants tax. Gains on property that has been held for more than five years are taxed at 20%: a 15% national tax plus a 5% local inhabitants tax. To calculate the five-year period, count backward from January 1 of the year the property was sold. For example, if you buy a property on January 2, 2009, and sell it on December 31, 2014, you will be taxed at the 39% rate.

Capital gains made by nonresidents of Japan are not subject to the 9% or 5% local inhabitants tax.

A tax deduction of up to ¥30 million is available on capital gains from the sale of your principal residence. To claim this deduction, you must have been the registered occupant for one of the past three years.

Additional relief is available if you buy a new principal residence within two years of selling your old residence.

Capital losses

Individual investors can only offset capital losses against similar capital gains recorded in the same tax year. If an owner-occupier buys a new home, he may carry a capital loss forward for up to three years and use it to offset other income.

Rental income

For residents, rental income from property in Japan is generally included with the owner's other income and taxed at the current marginal rate.

For nonresidents, rental income is generally subject to a 20% withholding tax, which is treated as a prepayment of the investor's tax bill. Nonresident investors are required to file a tax return but do not have to pay local taxes.

If you are a citizen of another country, that country may tax rental income or capital gains from the sale of property in Japan. However, you may be able to claim a credit for taxes paid in Japan (see "Residency" above).

Deductions and allowances

Insurance and improvements

Earthquake insurance premiums are tax-deductible and tax credits are available for improvements that make your home barrier-free, more energy efficient or increase its ability to withstand earthquakes. There is also a tax credit for homes damaged in officially recognized natural disasters.

Interest

Interest on loans used to buy income-producing property is deductible, but only for the portion of the loan represented by the building. For example, if you buy a property for ¥20 million, with the land valued at ¥15 million and the building at ¥5 million, 25% of the interest paid would be deductible.

Mortgages

The national government offers a 1.0% credit on the balance of mortgages for normal houses and 1.2% for "long-term quality houses." The credit is valid for a maximum of 10 years and is available to taxpayers who start residing in the home between 2009 and 2013. The maximum mortgage amount declines from ¥50 million in 2009 to ¥20 million in 2013 for normal houses and from ¥50 million to ¥30 million for long-term quality houses.

Solar power

In March 2009, the national government announced subsidies of ¥70,000 per installed kilowatt of solar power. Incentives are also available from 24 prefectures and several hundred local governments. To apply for the subsidies, see your prefectural and local government office and the Japan Photovoltaic Expansion Center (www.j-pec.or.jp, Japanese only).

Suspended taxes

Land price tax

The land price tax came into effect on January 1, 1992, for individuals and businesses owning land in Japan on January 1 each year. This national tax was suspended in 1998.

Special landholding tax

A special landholding tax, payable by individuals and businesses acquiring or holding land, was introduced in 1973. This municipal tax was suspended in fiscal 2003.

Tax-efficient structures

Investors can use a legal entity such as a *tokumei kumiai* (TK) or *tokutei mokuteki kaisha* (TMK) to reduce their tax liability. TKs and TMKs involve extra cost and complexity and must be structured correctly to ensure they withstand the scrutiny of the tax authorities. These structures are usually inappropriate for individuals with one or two properties.

Tokumei kumiai

In a TK, an individual or company invests in a Japan-based real estate operator in exchange for a share of the operator's profits. TK investors are silent partners with no direct control of the operator's business.

TK distributions to nonresident investors are subject to a 20% withholding tax. This tax is final and nonresident investors are not required to file an income tax return in Japan. In some circumstances, it is possible to structure a TK so distributions to nonresident investors are exempt from withholding tax.

Tokutei mokuteki kaisha

A TMK is a special-purpose vehicle used to securitize real estate and other assets. TMKs are usually used for large transactions, and shareholders in a TMK benefit from limited liability.[8]

SPECIAL CASES

A CUSTOM-DESIGNED HOME

With prices starting at about ¥1 million per *tsubo* (3.3 square meters), plus land, custom-designed homes are expensive. Planning and building a custom home can easily take two years and require thousands of decisions. The results, however, can be spectacular.

To build a custom home, you will need the services of an architect (*kenchikushi*). In addition to planning and designing your home, an architect can arrange bids, negotiate with contractors and suppliers and supervise the construction process. An architect can also help you achieve your environmental goals, make the most of an unusual building site, overcome drainage problems and ensure your home complies with shadow restrictions (*nichiei kisei*) and other regulations.

Defining the project

Building a custom home starts with a budget, which will include land, design and construction, furniture and appliances, taxes, insurance, maintenance and contingencies. A realistic budget will prevent you from running out of money halfway through the project or building something that you cannot afford to occupy.

Next, decide what you want. This includes physical and functional requirements, such as the home's overall size, the number of bathrooms (most Japanese homes only have one) and bedrooms, and your storage and parking needs. Consider your hobbies and interests and whether you will want a home theater, home office, gourmet kitchen, garden or basement. Think about the future, especially if you plan to have children or if your kids will be moving out. List your aesthetic preferences: Do you want a modern or traditional design? Finally, address environmental issues, such as rainwater collection or the use of solar power. These factors may also influence your choice of a site.

Understanding your needs, wants and preferences will help you find an architect whose style and experience are compatible with your vision. This process will also form the basis for the brief (see below) that you will use to explain your project to the architect.

Hiring an architect

When you have defined your priorities, start looking for an architect. You can find a list of practitioners, with photos of their work and contact information, at www.japan-architects.com. The Japan Institute of Architects (www.jia.or.jp) and Japan Federation of Architects & Building Engineers Association (www.kenchikushikai.or.jp, Japanese only) should also be helpful.

Assemble a short list of candidates and contact them. Describe your project, goals, schedule and budget. If the firm is interested and has capacity to work on your project, arrange a meeting. Talking to three to five firms will give you a sense of what is possible, without consuming too much time.

A meeting will let you review the firm's technical credentials, design philosophy and attitude toward customer service. Ask if the firm has professional liability insurance; many in Japan do not. Meet the architect who will design your home—not just the salesperson—so you can gauge the chemistry between you. Good chemistry is vital, because you and the architect will spend a lot of time together and it will not be pleasant or productive if you dislike or distrust each other. Check to see if there is a gap between your Japanese and the architect's English skills. Ask for references, talk to previous clients and visit the architect's finished projects. Smart architects interview their clients, so don't be surprised if she asks to visit your building site or your home. As part of the selection process, you may ask the architect to prepare preliminary sketches for which you will be charged a fee. Finally, ask how the architect charges for her work: as a percentage of the total building cost (excluding land), on an hourly basis or as a lump sum.

When you have selected an architect, notify her and the unsuccessful candidates as soon as possible. The winning architect will ask you to sign a contract, which will specify the schedule and the services she will provide. Depending on how the contract is structured, you will make four to six payments over the life of the project. Typically, there is a small initial payment for preliminary work, several larger ones as the project progresses and a small, final payment when minor defects and outstanding issues are resolved.

The brief

A well-organized, unambiguous brief is the foundation of a successful project. Use words, sketches, pictures from books and magazines, videos, paint samples, fabric swatches and anything else that conveys your goals and intentions. The more detail, the better.

Producing an effective brief takes time and effort. But with a clear brief, the architect will understand what you want and achieve your goals more quickly and efficiently. Creating the brief will help you clarify your thinking and may uncover gaps between your and your spouse's preferences. These differences are best resolved early in the design process, before changes become expensive.

In addition to your functional requirements and aesthetic preferences, tell the architect what features you consider essential and which ones are negotiable. If you are unsure about something, say so. Don't forget to give the architect creative "breathing space," so she can use her training and skill to turn your vision into a home you can both be proud of.

Other considerations

Since the 2005 discovery that architect Hidetsugu Aneha had faked earthquake-resistance data for 99 buildings, the process for approving building plans has become more strict. According to Astrid Klein of Klein Dytham architecture (www.klein-dytham.com) in Tokyo, it now takes 35–70 days to have designs approved by the government, up from 21 days before the Aneha scandal. When your plans have been accepted, only minor changes to items such as finishes are allowed. Previously, architects could simultaneously send project plans to tender and for approval, and then amend the plans after they were accepted. This is another reason to avoid changes late in the design process.

It can be difficult to arrange financing for a custom home, because many banks will not provide a mortgage for vacant land. In addition, banks sometimes see a mortgage on a custom home as having higher risk, believing the home's one-of-a-kind design will make it harder to sell if you default.

Companies specializing in the design and installation of kitchens operate in Japan. Western-style kitchens and appliances are available from Gaggenau (www.gaggenau.com), Miele (www.meile.com), Poggen Pohl (www.poggenpohl.com), Snaidero (www.snaidero.com) and Valcucine (www.valcucine.it), among others.

Custom designing your home allows you to build in a variety of technologies, including Category 5 or Category 6 Ethernet cable for a computer network, satellite TV and speaker cable for a home theater and an intercom or a burglar alarm. By law, fire alarms incorporating heat sensors or smoke detectors must be installed in homes built after June 1, 2006. The design stage is also a good time to consider installing extra electrical outlets and telephone jacks.

Green buildings

Japan's dependence on imported energy, coupled with rising oil prices and heightened environmental awareness, has given added impetus to the green building movement.

Previously, green buildings cost more to design and erect than conventional structures. That cost differential is narrowing, as architects and construction companies gain experience. Environmental technologies such as photovoltaic cells are becoming cheaper, more efficient and more reliable. National, prefectural and local governments offer subsidies to homeowners who install solar power systems and utility companies buy surplus electricity from solar panels in homes, schools and hospitals. Despite these advances, architect Mark Dytham notes that many people ask for green features in their initial designs, but drop them when they see the cost.

As green buildings have joined the mainstream, their benefits have become more pronounced. By combining energy-efficient designs, abundant natural light, zoned temperature controls and excellent indoor air quality, green buildings cost less to operate than conventional designs. In a year-long study in the U.S., tenants in green commercial buildings reported an average of 2.88 fewer sick days and more than half of respondents said employee productivity had increased. Companies are willing to pay more for green space, which they see as an aid to employee retention. The same report also found green buildings had 3.5% lower vacancy rates and 13% higher rental rates than their peers, making them attractive to landlords.[1]

Corporate sustainability strategist Charles Lockwood believes that green building techniques can be used in all
buildings. But rather than using experimental technologies,
he recommends proven, relatively inexpensive solutions like
adding thermal insulation and installing double-glazed windows. Replacing incandescent light bulbs with light-emitting
diode (LED) or compact fluorescent lamps results in an 80%
energy savings, and recent research has dismissed concerns
that the energy needed to manufacture LED lamps negates
their environmental benefits.[2]

While it is possible to retrofit buildings, it is generally cheaper
and easier to use an environmentally friendly design from
the start. One way to do this is through the Comprehensive
Assessment System for Building Environmental Efficiency
(CASBEE), a set of tools that rates a building's environmental
quality and performance, as well as its impact on the external
environment. CASBEE spans a building's life cycle from pre-
design and new construction to existing buildings and renovation, and includes English-language checklists. For more
information, see www.ibec.or.jp/CASBEE.

Architects in Japan

Japan is home to many internationally renowned architects, including Tadao Ando (www.tadao-ando.com), Shigeru Ban (www.
shigerubanarchitects.com) and Toyo Ito (www.toyo-ito.co.jp). Japan
also has a history of attracting talented practitioners from abroad.
In the late 1880s, Josiah Conder designed the main gallery of the
National Museum in Tokyo and was elected honorary president of the
Architectural Institute of Japan (www.aij.or.jp). Frank Lloyd Wright,
who opened an office in Japan in 1915, was responsible for several homes in Tokyo as well as the Imperial Hotel. More recently, Le
Corbusier designed the National Museum of Western Art in Tokyo.[3]
Today, numerous foreign architects practice in Japan. For a partial
list, see the Japan chapter of the American Institute of Architects
(http://aiajapan.org).

In Japan, architects work for two broad categories of employers.
The first is the big organizations that build big projects. This group
includes Japan's largest architectural firm, Nikken Sekkei Ltd. (www.
nikken.co.jp), which employs 872 first-class architects and designed
the Tokyo Midtown redevelopment project. Large construction

companies also have in-house architects, which helps the companies win jobs by bundling design and construction services. Construction companies usually focus on delivering practical, low-maintenance structures at a competitive price, rather than setting new aesthetic standards.

The second group comprises ateliers, most of which have fewer than 30 staff. Ateliers are design-driven firms with a signature style shaped by the founder or founders, whose names are often on the front door. Ateliers focus on smaller projects, such as stores, public buildings and individual homes. Both Japanese and foreign architects are well represented among the ateliers.

There are three classes of architect—first, second and wooden structure (*mokuzo*)—which detemine the projects the architect is able to undertake. Architects may work as a representative of the construction company or the building owner.

Contractors and architects

In Japan, design and construction services are often bundled into a single package that takes advantage of a longstanding relationship between an architect and contractor. Knowledge of each other's staff, approach and philosophy allows the two companies to start work quickly without the "getting to know you" phase that is common in new partnerships.

The drawback to this arrangement is that the client is quoted a single price for design and construction services, which can be disconcerting for customers expecting a clear demarcation between the two. Not all architects and contractors work this way, but it is common even for individual houses.

Design and construction work was often undertaken using a simple written order or even a verbal agreement. Recently, the use of contracts has become more frequent and the contracts have become more detailed. But contracts continue to be regarded as a statement of intent rather than a checklist that covers every possible eventuality. In Japan, relationships are important and agreements assume that if there is a problem, a solution will be reached that is fair to both parties.[4]

During the planning and construction phases, the line between architects and contractors can become blurred. It is not unusual for Japanese architects to spend time on-site, inspecting the construction and liaising with suppliers. Contractors, on the other hand, make design suggestions that save time and money and reduce risk. Project deadlines are often seen as targets. Compliance within a few days is usually acceptable as long as the other party is not inconvenienced.

Many architects' designs test the boundaries of what is technically possible. Contractors—who must implement architects' ideas and make a profit—tend to be conservative. However, in Japan the relationship between architects and contractors and between contractors and subcontractors is usually cordial and cooperative. This is in stark contrast with the United States and other countries where litigation and antagonism are the norm.

This cooperative approach reflects Japan's nonconfrontational culture and its legal system, which is based on civil law and where the outcome of a mediated settlement is usually very close to one delivered by the courts. Mediated settlements have the added advantage of arriving faster and at a much lower cost.

Alternatives

There are several alternatives for people who want a distinctive home but prefer not to hire an architect. These approaches are complicated and require hands-on involvement.

One option is to purchase building plans from a company such as Hometta (www.hometta.com) or Houseplans (www.houseplans.com), import or buy building materials in Japan and hire a contractor to erect the house for you. Plans start at about $1,000, and a variety of designs are available. Another company, FreeGreen (www.freegreen. com), offers both free and paid designs and provides editable CAD (computer-aided design) files so the plans can be customized. This approach requires a contractor who is comfortable working from Western-style drawings and adapting the design to meet Japanese regulations and conditions.

Wooden kit homes, which are known in Japan as log houses, are another option. Lindal Cedar Homes (www.lindal.com and www. lindaljapan.com, Japanese only), Sweden House (www.swedenhouse. co.jp, Japanese only) and other companies import these kits from Canada, Finland, Sweden and the United States. Many importers offer assembly services, but you can erect these homes yourself or hire a contractor to do it for you. It is also possible to buy log houses directly from manufacturers such as Lake Country Log Homes (www.lakecountrylog.com) in Canada. See "Log houses" for more information.

Finally, if you have the time and are looking for an adventure, you can design and build your own home. See "Build it yourself" in the "Resources" section for more information.

Zoning

The following zoning restrictions apply to land in urbanization promotion areas.[5] Variations are possible if the structure complies with the Building Standard Law.[6]

Zoning regulations were introduced after mixed land use was in place. As a result, regulations tend to be flexible and focus on maintaining the current land use pattern.[7]

Under Japanese zoning regulations, it is not unusual for homes to be located next to commercial and industrial concerns.

Urban zoning	
Zone	**Permitted uses**
Category I: Exclusive low-rise residential	Houses; small shops and offices; schools; temples, shrines and churches; clinics.
Category II: Exclusive low-rise residential	As above, plus shops and restaurants up to 150m².
Category I: Mid/high-rise residential	As above, plus hospitals and universities; shops and restaurants up to 500m²; independent garages up to 300m².
Category II: Mid/high- rise residential	As above, plus shops, restaurants and offices up to 1,500m².
Category I: residential	As above, plus shops, restaurants, offices and hotels up to 3,000m²; auto repair shops up to 50m².
Category II: residential	As above, plus karaoke lounges.
Quasi-residential	As above, plus theaters under 200m²; warehouses; garages up to 300m², auto repair shops up to 150m².
Neighborhood commercial	As above, plus theaters over 200m², shops and restaurants over 10,000m²; auto repair shops up to 300m².
Commercial	As above, plus bathhouses with private rooms.
Quasi-industrial	As above, plus factories posing some danger or environmental risk. Bathhouses are excluded.
Industrial	Houses; temples, shrines and churches; clinics; shops, offices and restaurants; karaoke lounges; garages; warehouses; auto repair shops; factories posing a strong risk of danger or environmental degradation.
Exclusive industrial	Shrines, temples and churches; offices; karaoke lounges; garages; warehouses; auto repair shops; factories posing a strong risk of danger or environmental degradation.
Areas without a designation	All of the above, except bathhouses with private rooms and theaters, shops and restaurants over 10,000m².

Custom built in Tokyo

In 2004, California native John Kirch and his Japanese wife, Chiharu, decided it was time to become homeowners.

John and Chiharu looked at neighborhoods in and around Tokyo for about a year before a Japanese friend introduced them to Shimouma in Setagaya-ku. Shimouma is a green, quiet area with more than 10 parks within a 10-minute bicycle ride, including Setagaya Park with its miniature steam engines and Komazawa Olympic Park, which was a site for the 1964 Olympic Games. Most of the homes in the area are two or two-and-a-half stories tall, and Shimouma has convenient public transit links, with Shibuya Station just two stops away on the Toyoko train line. With a well-stocked supermarket, several excellent restaurants, a neighborhood pub and three bakeries nearby, John describes Shimouma as "one of the best neighborhoods I've found in Tokyo."

Before the Kirchs were introduced to Shimouma, they used a shotgun approach to learn more about homes and housing. They read books and magazines, talked to friends and family and attended seminars organized by the American Chamber of Commerce in Japan (www.accj.or.jp) and by architect Kisho Kurokawa (www.kisho.co.jp), who designed the Nakagin Capsule Tower and National Arts Center in Tokyo. This shaped their thinking and helped them determine what they wanted in their new home.

After the Kurokawa seminar, the Kirchs began considering the relationship between their future home, the family's needs and the activities—such as barbeques, bicycle and ski outings and John's passion for motorcycles—that make up their lifestyle. After discussions with Chiharu's parents, they looked at the long-term implications of their choices and how to find a house that they could grow into over time.

As a result, the Kirchs decided they didn't want to pay condominium fees, which topped ¥100,000 a month for some properties. John was also keen to avoid the drawbacks of apartment living, especially for their son Christopher, who was born in 2003. "I wanted a garden outside where Chris could play whenever he wanted," says John.

The Japanese capital offers everything from small apartments to luxury condominiums and detached homes.

That meant a house and John viewed several existing homes, including one where the owners refused to let him perform a prepurchase structural survey, without finding anything that fit his family's requirements. He briefly considered erecting a log house, but felt the cost savings did not justify the design compromises that would be required. John even looked into moving an old house down from the mountains, an idea that was ultimately rejected as too expensive and impractical. In the end, a new home built to the family's specifications was the best solution.

Through an ad in a real estate magazine, John met an agent from Unihouse (www.unihouse.co.jp, Japanese only), who showed him a vacant plot in a neighborhood near Shimouma. While the property wasn't a good fit, the agent's willingness to understand John's preferences and find something suitable convinced John to continue working with him.

That proved to be a smart decision, as the agent later found an affordable 50-tsubo lot on a quiet cul-de-sac in Shimouma. "I got lucky," says John with a smile, noting that the land, which represented about two-thirds of the project's budget, has appreciated significantly since he bought it in 2005.

John spoke to several banks about a mortgage, a process he found frustrating. "I had one banker tell me, 'I'm sorry, we don't make loans on property, only on property with buildings on it. Once you build something on it, you can get a loan from us.'" In the end, the real estate agent introduced him to Sumitomo Mitsui Banking Corporation. "SMBC rolled out the red carpet for us. They made us feel welcome and comfortable coming to ask them for a little bit of money," he says. With a 50% down payment, it took less than three weeks to arrange the mortgage.

While the agent was searching for a suitable lot, the Kirchs were busy planning their new home. They met and interviewed several architects before settling on Isa Homes (www.isahomes.co.jp, Japanese only), a company that had been recommended by their real estate agent. John and Chiharu say they liked the employees' communication skills, dedication and the quality of the homes they had designed for other clients. Isa Homes helped the Kirchs maximize the floor space and height of their new home, while ensuring that it complied with the shadow restrictions, which prevent people from erecting buildings that leave their neighbors permanently in the shade.

The architect also incorporated a fireplace into the Kirchs' design, a late change that added about ¥2 million to the project cost and required structural reinforcements, heat proofing and a chimney. John says he was glad he added the fireplace, which he uses frequently during the winter months.

One of John's few regrets is not having a basement. Although it would have added approximately ¥2.5 million to the budget, the architects advised him that it could cause problems with mold, mildew and water leakage. "Having a foosball, pool or ping-pong table in the basement is very appealing, especially when it's pouring rain outside," notes John.

The architect agreed to separate the design and construction aspects of the project. John wanted separate contracts to ensure he was getting the best price and to provide transparency. He also had a local attorney review both contracts.

John interviewed and received quotes from several general contractors before settling on one recommended by Isa Homes. After initially submitting the most expensive quote, the architect's contractor produced a more competitive bid. John hired the contractor based on the lower bid, the contractor's close working relationship with the architect and the temple-grade carpentry he had seen at the contractor's other projects.

Before construction began, John arranged a traditional Shinto ceremony, known as a *jichinsai*, to purify the land, pacify the spirits, protect the workers from injury and prevent the building from being affected by structural problems.[8]

As construction progressed, John maintained a contingency fund to pay for changes like the new fireplace. He also received monthly updates from the contractor, who provided a 10-year guarantee on his work, which is standard under the Housing Quality Assurance Act. Six months later, the Kirchs' house was delivered on time and on budget.

Three years after moving in, the family remains happy with their home. John, who is working with the same real estate agent to find a second property, offers the following advice to potential home buyers:

- Think long and hard about what you need and want in your new home. When you are spending that much money, you really should get what you want. But that will not happen unless you understand your needs and desires.

- Find a real estate agent who you are comfortable with, who knows your target neighborhood and who listens to you, and then give him a clear brief and a budget.

- As long as you are making progress, stick with the agent, even if you do not like the first few properties he shows you.

- Get a good local lawyer to review the contracts.

- Maintain open communication with your agent, architect and contractor. Have a contingency fund of about 10% of the house's total projected cost. This will cushion you against unforeseen problems and last-minute changes.

- Hold regular meetings with your architect during the planning and design process. A 90-minute session every two weeks should be sufficient to review the architect's progress and make structural and design decisions.

INVESTMENT PROPERTY

As a resident or nonresident, you can buy and hold investment property in Japan. However, Japan's rental market and regulatory environment have several distinctive characteristics that will shape your investment approach.

The residential rental market

Renting is a popular choice in Japan. In 2008, rented homes represented 38.8% of all occupied dwellings. Rental rates vary by region: 48.7% of homes in Tokyo and 21.0% of those in Akita Prefecture were rented. Nationwide, 75.7% of the rental housing was privately owned, while 76.2% of the rental homes in Tokyo were privately held.[1]

Rental homes are small. In 2008, owner-occupied dwellings had an average size of 120.9 square meters, versus 45.9 square meters for rented ones. At 78.3 square meters, detached houses for rent had 60.0% of the floor space of owner-occupied houses, while rental apartments were only 57.1% as large as owner-occupied apartments.[2] Single people and couples often live in a rented dwelling. But when couples start a family, they must buy a home in order to have space for their children.

The need to pay "key money" and limits on landlords' ability to raise rents (see below) discourage people from moving. Only 8.3% of Japanese renters move each year, compared with 25.6% in the United Kingdom and 30.1% in the United States.[3] Peak moving season in Japan is from January to March.[4]

Renting in Japan

Renting a home in Japan is expensive. Before a tenant moves in, he pays between four and six months' rent, which breaks down as follows:

- Key money (*reikin*), which is a nonrefundable "gift" to the landlord equal to one or two months' rent.

- Deposit (*shikikin*) of one or two months' rent. This is refunded at the end of the tenancy, less any cleaning and repair charges.

- Agent's commission (*chukai tesuryo*) of one month's rent, plus consumption tax.

- The first month's rent.

- Property insurance, which typically costs ¥10,000–¥20,000 for a two-year lease. This is optional on smaller properties.

- A lock replacement fee, which typically costs ¥10,000–¥20,000.[5] This is also optional on smaller properties.

In what are known as "zero-zero" rentals, some landlords do not charge key money or a deposit. To offset the revenue shortfall, the landlord increases the monthly rent.[6]

In exchange for high initial costs, Japanese tenants enjoy considerable legal protection. However, as in most aspects of Japanese life, real estate disputes are usually resolved through discussion, not legal channels. The vast majority of Japanese tenants are responsible and law abiding; most issues between landlord and tenant are resolved quickly and amicably.

Most homes are rented using a regular lease (*futsu shakuya keiyaku*), which does not have a fixed termination date. A regular lease is automatically renewed, even if there is no renewal agreement. Rents are set at the beginning of the tenancy, but tenants may request a reduction if the rent is later found to be above market rates.[7] When a lease is renewed, the rent may not exceed the rent for a new lease on a comparable home. If a sitting tenant refuses to accept a rent increase, the case can go to court. While this is not a common occurrence, courts generally find in favor of the tenant.[8]

There are few justifications, such as nonpayment of rent, for a landlord to evict a tenant. The eviction process is difficult, time-consuming and expensive. Often, landlords pay tenants substantial amounts of money to leave.[9]

This regulatory environment provides a disincentive for owners to improve or redevelop their properties and can cause problems for landlords trying to recoup the cost of essential repairs, such as seismic reinforcements.[10] It also creates a business opportunity for the yakuza, who unscrupulous owners hire to force tenants to move.

Residential lease terms

A regular lease typically includes the following terms:

- The lease is for a two-year term. (The lease is automatically extended at the end of the term.)

- The tenant may terminate the lease with 30 days' notice or by paying rent in lieu of notice.

- Rent is payable on the last business day of the preceding month (i.e., February's rent is payable on the last weekday in January). Rent is usually paid by bank transfer.

- The landlord and tenant may enter discussions to revise the rent if the rent becomes unreasonable because of changes in property values, taxes or economic factors, or if the rent is inappropriate in relation to other buildings in the vicinity.

- The tenant agrees to pay the monthly condominium management fee. (This is usually paid to the landlord, who pays it and the building repair fee to the owners' committee each month.)

- The tenant may not alter the interior of the property.

- At the end of the lease, the tenant must return the property to the landlord in its original condition. The tenant is not responsible for wear and tear caused by normal use.

- The landlord is responsible for keeping the property in habitable condition. The tenant is responsible for any damage he causes; for replacing damaged shoji and tatami mats and burned-out light bulbs and fuses; and similar minor repairs.

- The tenant may not sublet the property.

- People who are not listed on the lease are not allowed to occupy the property.

- The tenant agrees to use the property only for residential purposes. (This clause can be negotiated, as apartments are often used as offices for small businesses.)

- The tenant agrees to pay the landlord a security deposit, which the landlord agrees to promptly return to the tenant at the end of the tenancy. The tenant may not use the deposit to offset outstanding rent or condominium management fees. Interest is not payable on the deposit. At the end of the tenancy, the landlord may deduct the cost of cleaning and repairs from the deposit. If these costs are deducted from the deposit, the landlord must give the tenant a breakdown of the expenses.

- The tenant may not do anything that will annoy or endanger other tenants.

- The landlord may cancel the lease if the tenant fails to pay the rent or condominium management fees or violates any of the other terms of the lease.

- The tenant will notify the landlord if the home will be vacant for one month or more.

- The tenant may not place personal items, signs or advertisements in the building's common areas.

- With the tenant's prior approval, the landlord may enter the property to conduct maintenance and repairs and to show the home to prospective tenants.* The tenant may not withhold reasonable requests for access by the landlord.

- The landlord may enter the property without the tenant's prior approval in an emergency, such as to prevent the spread of a fire. The landlord must advise the tenant of any such entry.

- The tenant's guarantor is jointly responsible for any unpaid rent, condominium management fees or damage.

- Issues not addressed above will be handled in accordance with the Japanese Civil Code, and other laws and trade practices for the real estate industry. The landlord and tenant will discuss and try to resolve any disputes through good-faith consultations.[11]

In 2000, fixed-term leases (teiki shakuya keiyaku) were introduced. A fixed-term lease is similar to a regular lease, except that it is not automatically extended at the end of the term. While a regular lease may be written or oral, a fixed-term lease must be in writing and include a separate, notarized document stating that the lease will not be renewed and will end when it expires. The landlord may terminate a fixed-term lease by giving the tenant 6–12 months' written notice. With the agreement of the tenant, it is possible to change a regular lease to a fixed-term lease. In 2007, less than 13% of detached home and 5% of condominium leases carried a fixed term.[12]

For both regular and fixed-term leases, the real estate agent reads an explanation of important matters (juyou jikou setsumeisho) to the tenant.[13] This document describes the property; outlines the facilities and equipment that are included in the property and their condition; explains the terms of the tenancy; and identifies the landlord, real estate agent and property manager. The tenant signs the explanation to indicate that he understands and agrees to the terms in it.

In Kyushu and the Kansai and Tokai regions, it is common for a restoration fee (shikibiki) to be automatically deducted from the deposit at the end of the tenancy. The fee is deducted even if the home is returned to the landlord in pristine condition.

*According to one source, asking a tenant for permission to show their home to a prospective tenant would be seen as extremely rude.

Lease renewal fees (*koshinryo*) of up to two months' rent are also common in Tokyo and Kyoto and in Shiga and Fukuoka prefectures. In July 2009, a Kyoto District Court ruled that these charges, which the landlord typically splits with the real estate agent,[14] were illegal.[15] In a separate case, in August 2009 the Osaka High Court upheld an earlier ruling in favor of a man who sued his landlord for the return of renewal fees he had paid for his Kyoto apartment.[16] The full effects of these rulings are not yet clear. Most Japanese tenants continue to pay renewal fees, while some expatriates try to exclude them when negotiating a lease. If, as a landlord, you plan to collect renewal fees, it is essential that this is explicitly stated in the explanation of important matters.

Landlords normally insist that tenants provide a guarantor (*hoshonin*), who will be responsible if the tenant damages the property, or fails to pay the rent or condominium management fee. Typically, the tenant's parents (regardless of the parents' age, income or employment status) or employer act as the guarantor. Increasingly, renters without family or a full-time job turn to rental guarantee companies (*yachin hosho kaisha*), which provide this service. The companies charge 30%–100% of the monthly rent for a two-year lease. This is not insurance: If the tenant defaults, the guarantee company pays the landlord and pursues the tenant for the outstanding money.[17] According to one estimate, about 40% of renters use these companies.[18]

Open-ended leases and complex eviction procedures make landlords cautious. Before renting a home, prospective tenants must complete a detailed application form, which lists their personal data, income, employment history, rental history, guarantor and the names of the people who will be living in the property.

Difficult tenants

The elderly, the disabled, foreigners and families with small children frequently have trouble finding rental accommodations. Landlords are reluctant to rent to these groups for a variety of reasons.

The elderly are more likely to die in a property, reducing its resale value. Often, elderly people are long-term residents who are unlikely to move out and allow the landlord to raise the rent. There are also concerns about old people having accidents, starting fires or becoming ill.[19]

Some disabled tenants require special facilities, such as barrier-free designs, while families with small children may damage the property or disturb the neighbors.

Foreigners may upset xenophobic neighbors and fail to observe local regulations, such as sorting garbage. Westerners have a reputation for throwing loud parties, while some landlords worry that Asian tenants will invite their extended family to move in with them.

There are several government and industry programs to assist tenants in these groups:

- The Trusted Renting Support Business (www.anshin-chintai.jp) includes real estate agents who serve elderly, foreign and disabled tenants, as well as families with small children.

- Through the Act for the Stable Living of the Elderly, the government guarantees elderly tenants' rental payments for up to six months.[20]

- The House Moving Scheme for the Elderly helps old people with large homes move into smaller rental units and lease their homes to families with children. The government guarantees the elderly owner will receive the rent from their tenant, thus giving them the confidence to move into a rental unit that better suits their needs.[21]

- The Japan Property Management Association operates a Website for foreigners called Welcome Chintai (http://welcome.jpm.jp) with information in Chinese, English, Korean, Mongolian, Spanish, Russian and German.

What and where to buy

For many renters, a small apartment near their workplace, shops and restaurants is preferable to a larger home and a long commute. In a 2003 survey by the Tokyo Metropolitan Government, 80% of respondents said one hour was the maximum tolerable commuting time.[22]

TOKYO RENTAL YIELDS

% PER YEAR

(Bar chart showing rental yields for 4LDK, 3LDK, 1LDK, 2LDK, 1R, 1K)

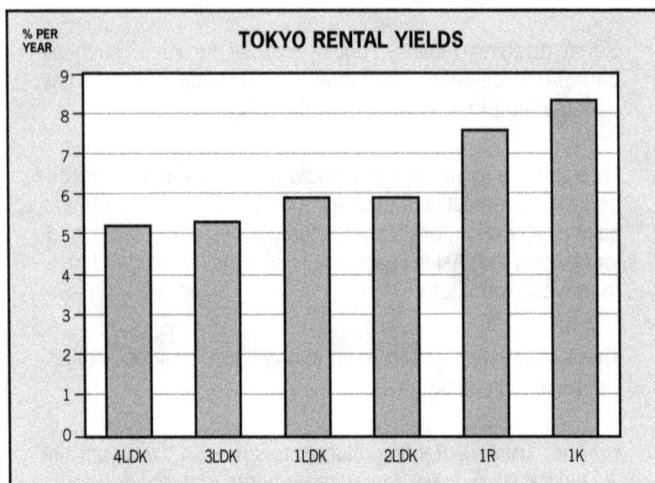

In general, small pre-owned apartments offer low risk and high returns. Medium-sized new and secondhand homes are low risk and low return. Large properties, such as family homes, are high risk and low return.[23] Luxury homes designed and equipped for expatriate families have been a poor investment since the financial downturn that started in September 2008. Rents are depressed because there is an oversupply of these properties and few new expatriates are moving to Japan.

As Akasaka Real Estate's Erik Oskamp observes, "There's usually an inverse relationship between a property's yield and its desirability as a home for an expat." In the Tokyo area, homes in desirable places like Kamakura and Kichijoji have lower rental yields than those in grittier neighborhoods like Ueno and Higashi Chiba.[24]

Look for homes that are bland, unexceptional, close to a train or subway station and near other residential complexes. These homes are easy for real estate agents and tenants to understand, which makes them simpler to rent and sell.

Government offices, universities and hospitals are recession-proof employers that create demand for rental housing. Universities and teaching hospitals have the added advantage of attracting students who will stay for a short tenancy, allowing you to raise rents when the economy improves.

Homes with tenants are desirable, because there is no need to pay a real estate agent to find one. However, if there is a sitting tenant you will almost certainly have to buy the apartment without seeing the interior, as tenants are not obliged to show their homes to prospective purchasers. In the current deflationary environment, there is also the risk that a sitting tenant will request a rent reduction. If she fails to obtain a reduction and moves out, you may still have to lower the rent for the next tenant.

If you buy a property with a sitting tenant, you assume the vendor's obligation to repay the tenant's security deposit. The buyer deducts the tenant's security deposit from the purchase price. Landlords do not have to pay interest on security deposits.

If you are buying an apartment, don't forget to check the annual report prepared by the building owners' committee, which will list the amount of money in the building's repair fund, major problems and long-term rehabilitation plans. You may also have to spend money on minor repairs to the inside of the apartment.

In Tokyo, prices per square meter for very small apartments tend to be high. Prices drop for units in the 35- to 100-square-meter range, and then increase for larger units. Newer units command a higher price than older ones, with 30- to 40-year-old apartments selling for significant discounts.[25]

Many real estate agents provide property management services. These range from basic plans to full-service packages that guarantee the landlord will receive the rent, even if the tenant doesn't pay.

The Foreign Exchange and Foreign Trade Act (Act No. 228 of 1949) requires nonresidents to file a "Report Concerning Acquisition of Real Property in Japan or Rights Related Thereto," with the Bank of Japan if they buy real estate for investment purposes.[26] The report must be filed within 20 days of the purchase and is not required if the property is used as a residence for the buyer, his relatives or employees; to house a business or nonprofit business; or if the property is purchased from another nonresident.[27]

Sample figures

These are actual costs for an 18.5-square-meter, one-room apartment in Tokyo's Meguro-ku. The apartment is one of 30 in a six-story building constructed from reinforced concrete in 1973. It is an eight-minute walk from the nearest train station, which is four minutes from Shibuya station. The apartment was purchased in December 2009.

Purchase		
Item	**Amount**	**% of total**
Purchase price	¥6,600,000	93.45
Judicial scrivener's fee	109,200	1.55
Brokerage fee	270,900	3.84
Stamp duty	10,000	0.14
Acquisition tax on building*	32,000	0.45
Acquisition tax on land*	40,800	0.58
Total	**¥7,062,900**	**100.00**

Annual income	
Item	**Amount**
Rent @ ¥76,500/month (¥70,000 rent + ¥6,500 condominium management fee)**	¥918,000
Property tax	-23,889
Condominium management fee (kanri-hi) @ ¥6,500/month	-78,000
Building repair fee (shuzen tsumitate kin) @ ¥1,300/month	-15,600
Management fee @ 5% of rent	-45,900
Total	**¥754,611**

Apartments in Tokyo

Growing up on a farm in rural Australia gave Simon Klassen a strong preference for urban living.

A finance professional who now lives in Hong Kong, Simon spent a total of eight years in Tokyo, most recently in 2006/7. In addition to speaking and reading Japanese, Simon is comfortable buying property across borders. He acquired a Singapore shophouse in 2005 and an apartment in Shenzhen, China, during the SARS (sudden acute respiratory syndrome) outbreak in 2003.

* Acquisition tax is payable several months after the sale is completed. These figures are estimates.

** In this example, the tenant pays the landlord ¥6,500 per month in condominium management fees in addition to the rent. The landlord then pays the management fees to the building owners' committee.

Simon also owns two apartments in Tokyo, which were purchased through Akasaka Real Estate (www. akasakarealestate.com). Simon paid cash for the apartments, which were attractively priced in the Australian dollars he was holding.

Both units are under 30 square meters and over 10 years old. The apartments had tenants, which prevented Simon from inspecting the interiors before his purchase. However, Simon felt fortunate because he did not need to renovate either apartment.

Simon had no qualms about buying property in Japan because he knew other foreigners who had done so. "I also enjoyed walking around different neighborhoods and doing the research," he says. Initially, Simon managed the apartments. He later turned this role over to Akasaka Real Estate, which collects rent, pays property taxes and looks after maintenance and administration.

He bought the first apartment, in Shintomi near Ginza, for ¥9.5 million in late 2007. The apartment is one of 13 in the building, giving Simon a relatively large share of the land underneath. The building next door had recently been redeveloped, suggesting that Simon's building had redevelopment potential. By paying cash, he completed the transaction in one day.

Simon paid ¥17 million for the second apartment, which is in Nagatocho and a short walk from the prime minister's residence. Like the Shintomi apartment, this unit was built for residential use but had been rented to a commercial tenant— a common occurrence in Japan.

The Nagatocho purchase hit a snag when the vendor, the general manager of a Yokohama-based insurance company, requested two cashier's checks, one large and one small, payable to "cash." Simon's bank refused to issue the large check, citing money laundering regulations. When Simon told the vendor that the only alternative was several bricks of ¥10,000 notes, the vendor revealed the payees' names. It then became clear that the vendor was embarrassed because the large check was payable to a finance company and the much smaller check represented the vendor's profit.

Older apartments offer very basic facilities.

Simon suspects the apartment, the interior of which was in pristine condition, had been rented by a middleman for a politician, who used it to hold meetings. When the tenant did not pay rent for three months, Simon enlisted Akasaka Real Estate to negotiate with the tenant on his behalf. The middleman then paid the outstanding three months' rent and an additional month in lieu of notice. Akasaka Real Estate then rented the apartment to a tenant the company found on Craigslist (http://tokyo.craigslist.jp).

Simon estimates his gross yield is 9.7% in Shintomi and 7.0% in Nagatocho. The total monthly fees, including the condominium management and building repair charges, are ¥16,000 in Shintomi and ¥13,000 in Nagatocho. While he doesn't think the yen value of either property has increased, both have done well in Australian dollar terms. Simon believes the Nagatocho apartment has greater appreciation potential because of its location, but would be happy to live in the Shintomi apartment. "Don't buy anything that you wouldn't want to live in," he advises.

Simon is partial to smaller apartments in older buildings, especially those near a train or subway station. Properties inside Tokyo's Yamanote train line are not much more expensive than those outside it and often attract higher rents from tenants seeking a shorter commute. But look closely at deals that offer an unusually high rate of return. "Apartments with very high yields carry a hidden burden somewhere," he says.

FORECLOSURES

In the United States, Canada and many other countries, buying fore-closed property is a well-established process. It is also possible in Japan, and the number of auctioned homes is growing as more people default on their mortgages because of the economic downturn that began in the fall of 2008.

Here is how to buy foreclosed property in Japan:

- Check the listings on the http://bit.sikkou.jp Website (Japanese only) or watch for the foreclosure notices published each month in the local newspaper. Typically, about half the foreclosed properties are detached homes and 20% are condominiums. Vacant land and commercial properties make up the balance.

- Next, visit the courthouse listed in the notice and complete a se-ries of forms that identify you, the property you want to buy and the amount of your bid.

- You will need to make a deposit—typically 10%–20% of the re-serve price set by the court—which is applied to the purchase price if your bid is successful. The deposit is refunded in full if your bid is unsuccessful, but is forfeited if you are the winning bidder and fail to complete the purchase. In some jurisdictions, the court retains the runner-up bidder's deposit until the winner has completed the purchase.

- A week after the end of the bidding period specified in the notice, the bids are opened in public. The highest bidder then has four to six weeks to pay the outstanding balance and purchase the property. Once the purchase is completed, it is final. The former owner cannot reclaim the property.

The process and all of the documents are in Japanese, so you will need to be fluent or get help from someone who is. You can also enlist the services of a company like Foreclosed Japan (www.foreclosedjapan.com), which maintains an English-language list of foreclosed properties and can guide you through the bidding process.

Steven Windholz, a consultant with Foreclosed Japan, says his company can provide market data to ensure that you don't over-bid, explain the documentation and associated terminology and help you complete the purchase. Foreclosed Japan also offers property management and other services for people purchasing investment property.

Banks are reluctant to offer mortgages on foreclosed property and many buyers pay cash. Steven says he has heard of people paying cash for a foreclosed property and then refinancing it, but has not made this arrangement for any of his clients.

The buying process has recently become simpler. For example, bidders no longer have to be permanent residents of Japan. In addition, the courts now maintain a file on the foreclosed property that includes photos of the interior, diagrams of the property and other information that can give a prospective buyer a better idea of the property's condition.

However, people buying foreclosed properties face several challenges:

- Japan is a mature real estate market. There are many knowledgeable, experienced investors with access to cash. As a result, the most desirable properties have usually been picked over by professional investors.

- Tenant protection laws prevent you from inspecting the property before you bid on it. These laws also make it difficult and time-consuming to evict tenants.

- The yakuza are active in real estate and frequently occupy buildings to depress auction prices.

It's important to have a clear understanding of what is and is not covered by the foreclosure process. Steven Windholz notes that if you buy a foreclosed property that has been rented out, you'll usually be responsible for returning the tenant's deposit at the end of their tenancy. You may also be expected to cover other unpaid fees.

Despite these challenges, Steven believes there is value in the market, noting that foreclosed properties in Tokyo, Yokohama and Osaka often sell for a 10% discount. Smaller, regional cities such as Sendai and Hiroshima offer potential discounts of up to 30%, while even bigger bargains can be found in rural areas.

While you don't want to overbid for a property, you'll waste a lot of time and effort if your bids are consistently too low. To avoid this problem, learn about the neighborhood, talk to local real estate agents and check the price of comparable properties displayed in agents' windows. You can also knock on the neighbors' doors and ask them what properties are selling for in their building. While not everyone will be willing to share this information, many people will be happy to help, especially if you are pleasant, polite and can speak Japanese.

Foreclosed property in Yamanashi

A 30-year resident of Japan who speaks fluent Japanese, American David Markle lives in a small town in Yamanashi Prefecture with his wife and children. Since 2004, he has bought five foreclosed properties—known as *keibai bukken*—including a farmhouse, undeveloped agricultural land and three apartments in "mansions," the Japanese term for upmarket, multistory residential buildings that are usually built using reinforced concrete.

David's first foreclosed property was an 800-*tsubo* (2,645 square-meter) site that included an old farmhouse; a second, smaller home; a garage; and several outbuildings. He bought the property, which had an estimated value of ¥8 million, for ¥1.5 million after his wife spotted a foreclosure notice in the newspaper.

David notes that the staff in his local courthouse were very helpful. "They answered our questions, helped us complete the paperwork and were very welcoming to us as nonprofessionals," he says.

After buying them for cash and finding stable tenants, David refinanced three of his properties. "I still own the properties and collect rent from them, which is paying off the mortgages and then some, and I get the benefits of having the cash available for doing other things," he says.

David and his wife, who is from the Kanto region, have lived in the area for about 10 years and appreciate the town's fresh air, good quality of life and access to services and transportation. However, he notes that outsiders are sometimes viewed with suspicion. The situation was exacerbated by the fact that David isn't Japanese and was buying foreclosed property—an activity that some see as shameful or disreputable.

"There was a sense of, 'Oh, what's going on here? What's this guy up to?'" says David, who admits to being anxious about how his neighbors would react to a foreigner buying foreclosed property. The situation was made more complicated because the former owners were living in the first foreclosed home he purchased.

David talked to a lawyer and considered a range of options, including coming to an agreement with the former owners or hiring someone to evict them. In the end, he let them stay in the house for three years rent free, until the husband died and the wife decided to move on. While this may not have been the most profitable approach, it did help to build goodwill with David's neighbors, something that can be important in a small, tightly knit community.

He had fewer difficulties with the three mansions he purchased. "The first one was kind of rundown, but not unlivable," he says. "It was empty, and we needed to put in new kitchen cabinets and repair one of the walls, but that was no big deal."

The second was fully furnished and slightly more complicated. "At the auction, I bought the property but not the furniture. So I called the former owners and asked them if they wanted to come and pick up their furniture. They said I'd have to pay them if I wanted to keep the furniture. I told them to send a truck over, and I'd help them load it. They hung up on me and I never heard from them again."

The third mansion was more of a textbook foreclosure, where the former owners walked away leaving dirty dishes in the sink. After giving the unit a thorough cleaning and making some minor repairs, David said he had no trouble finding a tenant.

Neighbors can also be an issue. At one point, David purchased agricultural land that had been rezoned as residential. The access road to the property was agricultural land that had never been rezoned as a road and the farmer who owned the land tried to charge David a fee to access his property. After several confrontations, David and the farmer ended up in mediation. Ultimately, the farmer backed down and let him use the road.

Despite these challenges, David believes it is still possible to find value in foreclosed property, especially if you do your research. He points out that you are competing with local investors and real estate agents who know how much things cost and are hoping to flip the property for a quick profit. If you are planning to use the property yourself, hold it for the long term or rent it out, you may be able to make a profit on a property that real estate agents pass up.

"Every situation is different," concludes David, "and it doesn't always go by the book. It helps to be prepared for the long haul and to be tenacious. If you don't expect everything to be perfect, you won't be disappointed."

NISEKO

Located in southwestern Hokkaido, about 90 kilometers from Sapporo, the Niseko resort area centers on the 1,308-meter Mount Niseko Annupuri. Closer to the town of Kutchan than to Niseko, the resort comprises the Annupuri, Higashiyama, Hirafu and Hanazono areas, all of which have gondola or ski lift access to Niseko Annupuri.

An emerging global destination

Niseko is famous for the quality and quantity of its snow. It's not unusual for snow to fall for 150 days each year and for 14 meters to accumulate over a season.[1] Deep, dry "champagne" powder, 48 kilometers of ski runs, 38 lifts and a long ski season have made Niseko especially popular with Australians, who are being joined by a growing number of visitors from China, Hong Kong, South Korea, Singapore and Taiwan.[2] During the 2006/7 season, Niseko attracted about 14,000 foreign visitors. That number grew to 24,000 in 2007/8.[3]

In addition to skiing and snowboarding, Niseko features summer activities such as horseback riding, hot-air ballooning, hiking and golf. Canoeing, fishing and whitewater rafting are available on the nearby Shiribetsu River, and the area offers numerous hot springs (*onsen*), which are a soothing place to relax after a day of skiing or hiking.

Niseko benefits from Japan's reputation as a safe destination and from awareness of Hokkaido's clean air and open spaces. Higher oil prices, which made flights from Asia to North America and Europe more expensive, work in Niseko's favor. Tougher visa requirements for many nationalities visiting or transiting the United States and the long lines and often inhospitable reception at America's airports have also helped. Finally, short flights and the absence of jet lag make Niseko well suited to the brief vacations that are common in Asia.

Niseko offers luxury, ski-in/ski-out condominiums.

The area's emergence as an international destination is relatively recent. In part, this is because Japan's tourism efforts have traditionally focused on serving domestic holidaymakers and outbound travelers rather than on welcoming inbound vacationers. This appears to be changing with the October 2008 launch of the Japan Tourism Agency and its goal of attracting 10 million inbound tourists in 2010.[4] And while Hokkaido is a popular destination for Japanese tourists, most visit during the summer.

The development of Niseko's tourism industry has been driven by a group of Australian pioneers who saw the area's potential and started businesses ranging from tour companies to real estate agencies. Many of these businesses are owner-operated and self-funded, because Japanese banks are often unwilling to lend to foreigners. The owners' frontline interaction with customers lets them react quickly to emerging opportunities. It also makes for a lively, dynamic environment for guests.

Niseko's growing popularity has attracted international investors. In September 2007, Pacific Century Premium Developments, a subsidiary of Hong Kong–based telecommunications company PCCW, acquired Nihon Harmony Resorts, which owned 180 acres of land in Niseko and had announced plans to build a large resort in the area. In March 2007, a unit of the U.S.-headquartered Citigroup bought the 506-room Niseko Higashiyama Prince Hotel from Seibu Holdings. After a multimillion-dollar refurbishment, the hotel reopened as the Hilton Niseko Village in July 2008. Several other large developments are planned.

Transportation

Access is an important consideration for any resort and Niseko is no exception. The vast majority of visitors arrive by air via Sapporo's New Chitose Airport, which offers flights to cities in Japan and to Beijing, Busan, Dalian, Guam, Hong Kong, Seoul, Shanghai, Taipei and Yuzhno-Sakhalinsk. In winter, there are also flights to Australia. It is 2.5 hours by bus and about 3 hours by train from New Chitose Airport to Niseko. Hokkaido Aviation Co. (www.hokkaido-koku.co.jp)[5] operates a helicopter service from Sapporo's Okadama Airport, while Aero Asahi Corporation (www.aeroasahi.co.jp) offers helicopter transfers from New Chitose Airport.[6]

Using a combination of bullet train (*shinkansen*), express and local trains, you can travel from Tokyo to Niseko in about 10 hours. East Japan Railways operates the overnight Hokutosei and Cassiopeia services between Tokyo's Ueno Station and Sapporo Station. In 2005, work began on a shinkansen line between Aomori in northern Honshu and Sapporo. Scheduled for completion by 2015, the line will include a stop in Kutchan and trim the travel time from Tokyo to Sapporo to approximately 4 hours.[7]

Most people arriving in Japan use Narita Airport, which currently has three flights per day to New Chitose Airport. Tokyo's main domestic airport, Haneda, has about 50 flights each day to Sapporo. Travelers arriving at Narita must either wait for a late morning or early evening flight to Sapporo, or take a bus (www.limousinebus.co.jp) from Narita to Haneda, a 75-minute journey that costs ¥3,000. More flights between Narita and Sapporo are reportedly being planned and Haneda is adding international connections, both of which will help to alleviate this bottleneck.

Niseko real estate

Developers have recently begun building properties for people who want to own a vacation home in Niseko. Custom-built and decorated to international standards, they include condominiums and houses that allow residents to walk out their front door and onto a ski lift. In the fall of 2009, condominiums in the Hirafu area started at approximately ¥40 million.

These properties are designed, built and marketed to investors who want to use them for one or two weeks each season and have a professional manager rent them out on a short-term basis during the rest of the year. Most are equipped like a serviced apartment, with furniture, bed linens and towels, pots and pans, large and small appliances, satellite TV, DVD player, stereo and broadband Internet.

Appliances with English controls are common and managers will prepare condensed English-language manuals to help guests operate equipment with Japanese labels.

Property management services are usually available from the company that built the house or condominium, or from a specialist property manager. Regardless of its affiliation, the manager should be licensed by the Ministry of Land, Infrastructure, Transport and Tourism.

Typically, managers offer a turnkey package. For 10%–25% of the gross rental income (usually with a fixed minimum annual fee), the manager handles everything from marketing and renting the units to maintenance and repairs. They can also pay bills and provide assistance with insurance, banking, local taxes and snow removal.

Unlike many small towns in Japan, English is widely spoken in Niseko. But it is not universal and people who don't speak Japanese may need help to accomplish relatively simple tasks, like filling up at a self-serve gas station. As a result, it's important to choose a manager who can offer support—such as meet-and-greet, shuttle bus and grocery shopping services; arranging airport transfers, lift tickets, ski lessons and babysitting; and looking after ski, mobile phone and car rentals—to guests renting your property.

If you plan to rent your chalet, ensure it is attractive to both property managers and potential guests. That means a convenient location on or very near the ski hill, an attractive design and decoration, a full complement of modern appliances and regular maintenance. It's possible to buy a property where some of these attributes are missing, but you may have difficulty finding a property manager, your unit may be last on the manager's rental list and revenues may be disappointing. Small, older chalets within driving distance of the ski lifts are available for as little as ¥10 million.

From a manager's perspective, an apartment in a new 10-unit condominium on the ski hill is easier to operate, market and rent than a lone chalet in a distant part of the resort. Large, one-of-a-kind luxury chalets in superior locations can command sufficiently high rents to make them attractive to a management company.

You can also custom build your chalet. There are foreigner-friendly contractors and architects in the area. Land prices start at about ¥10,000 per square meter and escalate rapidly as you get closer to the ski lifts.

Money

In the summer of 2008, international lenders, including Commonwealth Bank of Australia and National Australia Bank, began offering mortgages on properties in Niseko. This was significant because Japanese banks would not provide mortgages to nonresidents buying recreational property as an investment. As a result, almost all buyers paid cash. By the fall of 2009, however, both banks had withdrawn from this market.

Investors had hoped the availability of mortgages would help drive capital values, which had increased about 30% in 2006 and 2007, and rental rates, which had been growing at about 20% per year, higher still. Unfortunately, the arrival of the overseas banks was followed by a global credit crisis, sharp falls in international stock markets and steep increases in the value of the yen and U.S. dollar. The Australian dollar fell from about ¥98 in January 2008 to ¥57 in late October 2008, boosting the cost of a ¥40 million chalet from A$408,000 to over A$701,000. The Korean won and Singapore and Taiwan dollars also dropped against the yen, increasing prices for buyers from these countries.

Currency fluctuations also hurt owners' ability to rent their properties. During the 2007/8 season, for example, accommodations were in extremely short supply, especially during the peak Christmas, New Year and Lunar New Year periods. In late October 2008, one media report said that a large, unnamed hotel had seen 15% of its winter reservations canceled, mainly due to foreign exchange–related price increases. For the six months ended June 30, 2009, visitor arrivals to Japan fell 28.6% from a year earlier, to 3.1 million. Arrivals in February 2009 dropped 41.3% from a year earlier on the back of a global recession and concerns about H1N1 influenza.

In the current environment, anyone buying an offshore property—whether in Niseko or elsewhere—should be cautious. Test your financial assumptions against unfavorable exchange rate movements, higher interest rates and further deterioration in consumer sentiment. And if you are buying off the plan or signing a management contract, ensure the developer or property manager is financially sound.

Potential concerns

Despite Niseko's abundant snow, clean air and spectacular scenery, there are issues that potential buyers should consider.

Niseko aspires to be a five-star, international resort that can compete with Whistler or Vail. However, Niseko lacks basic tourist infrastructure. For example, the resort's first automated teller machine capable of accepting non-Japanese bankcards opened in the summer of 2009.[8] A 2006 report by the Japan External Trade Organization (JETRO) cited a shortage of restaurants and money-exchange facilities in Hirafu,[9] while some visitors have complained about a lack of hair salons and movie rental shops. High rents for retail space are also an issue.

Shopping—particularly for the global luxury brands found in high-end resorts—is limited. Niseko does not have a McDonald's, Starbucks or other international food and beverage outlet offering a fast, predictable (if uninspired) lunch for skiers wanting a break from Japanese food or from the local interpretation of Western dishes. And as mentioned above, getting to Niseko from Narita can be time-consuming.

None of these issues are necessarily deal breakers. But they could deter guests with children who are picky eaters; skiers looking for a homogenous, international experience; and people who want to deplane and go skiing as quickly as possible.

If you benchmark Niseko against other international resorts, property prices are reasonable, especially given the quality of the snow and proximity to major Asian cities. But Niseko is located in an area where, within a few kilometers of the ski hill, property prices are low and stagnant. And memories of Japan's property bust in the early 1990s remain vivid.

For the most part, Niseko remains a winter resort. That means rental revenues for your property during the off-season will range from low to zero. The tourism community is working to attract more visitors during the summer and, if they are successful, it should encourage the establishment and year-round operation of new tourist-oriented businesses. This could create a "virtuous circle" of new investments drawing more skilled workers, creating improved services, attracting additional tourists and so on.

Zoning is another concern. In 2007, Tokyo-based Zephyr Co. announced plans to build a 43-meter-tall condominium in Hirafu. The complex would have been nearly double the maximum height specified in local building guidelines, which were upgraded to an ordinance in March 2008. Zephyr tried to arrange an exception to the ordinance, but filed for bankruptcy protection in July 2008 with debts of ¥94.9 billion.[10]

Finally, much of the tourism development continues to be driven by Australian (as well as Canadian, British and American) expatriates. Inevitably, there are differences of opinion between the locals and expats on issues ranging from building colors to the opening hours of bars. A visit to the Kutchannel online forum (http://kutchannel.net) is an easy and often entertaining way to stay abreast of local issues.

A vacation home in Gunma

While Niseko is becoming an international destination to rival Whistler, Vail and St. Moritz, there are other ways to invest in and enjoy recreational property in Japan, as Dale Willetts and his wife, Alyssa, discovered.

The Willetts have never lived in Japan and don't speak Japanese, but they did spend several ski vacations in Niseko, starting at Easter 1999. "We had a great time," says Dale. "The snow was fantastic and the place was brilliant." They also found the trip from their home in Hong Kong was easier and less expensive than flying to a ski resort in Dale's native Canada.

Dale, Alyssa and their son, Benjamin, returned to Niseko several times until the area's growing popularity became a disadvantage. "We stopped going two or three years ago because you had to book a year ahead for Christmas or Chinese New Year," explains Dale, who also mentions rising hotel prices and difficulty in reserving direct flights from Hong Kong to Sapporo as drawbacks.

In 2007, the Willetts wanted a Christmas ski holiday. A friend told them about Minakami in Gunma Prefecture, where he owned a vacation home. Over Christmas, Dale and his wife rented a two-story mountain chalet in Minakami and—after a couple of days—decided to buy it. "It was exactly what we were looking for: peaceful and away from it all, yet very convenient to get to and reasonably priced," says Willetts.

A 75-minute shinkansen ride from Tokyo, the three-bedroom chalet sits on a 700-square-meter lot. Skiing, hiking, biking, rafting, paragliding and sport fishing are nearby, as are golf courses and numerous hot springs. The Willetts bought the chalet from a Japanese-speaking American, who built it in the 1970s.

Dale estimates the chalet cost about one-third of a comparable property in the Niseko area. He made a 10% deposit on signing the sale and purchase agreement and paid 50% three months later and the balance on registration. He paid cash for the chalet, because he felt his nonresident status would make it difficult to get a mortgage.

Several aspects of the transaction were unusual. Because the Willetts' friend knew the chalet's owner, the sale was completed without a real estate agent. The vendor introduced the Willetts to a local judicial scrivener (*shiho-shoshi*), who handled the transaction documents, which were scrutinized for the Willets by a Tokyo-based attorney. And since the buyer and seller were native English speakers, the sale and purchase agreement was written in English and then translated into Japanese. Both versions were then registered with the town office.

Alyssa, who is a furniture designer, imported a 40-foot container of furniture from China for the vacation home. She traveled to Japan and completed a declaration that the container was unaccompanied baggage, which allowed the furniture to be imported free of taxes and duties. Alyssa then gave the declaration to a freight forwarder, who handled the shipping arrangements.

One thing that Dale had not counted on was the need for a certificate of alien registration (*gaikokujin toroku genpyo kisai jikou shomeisho*). "It's impossible to open a bank account, register your utilities and arrange other services without one," he says. The certificate is not hard to get, but it takes up to 14 days to process the paperwork and you cannot leave Japan during that time.

Your passport will then indicate that you've received the certificate of alien registration and when you leave Japan you'll either need a re-entry permit or you'll have to surrender your certificate at the immigration counter. As Dale explains, "They will not issue a re-entry permit for a 90-day tourist visa. The result is that you are forced to give up the certificate the first time you leave the country after obtaining it."*

*In February 2009, the government announced plans to amend the Immigration Control and Refugee Recognition Act so that certificates of alien registration would be issued by the Ministry of Justice instead of municipal governments. Foreigners will be required to report changes in their address or place of employment to the Immigration Bureau and face significant fines if they fail to comply.

Unlike Niseko's turnkey approach, the Willetts' vacation home is a hands-on investment. Dale hired a local retiree as a caretaker and hopes to rent the chalet out to a family in Tokyo, an arrangement that will allow the Willetts to use it for several weeks each year while ensuring the chalet does not sit empty the rest of the time.

The Willetts family is happy with their vacation home and its four-season appeal. They also appreciate its proximity to Tokyo and the frequent flights between Hong Kong and Tokyo, which can be booked even during peak travel periods.

However, Dale counsels anyone contemplating a similar purchase to ensure they have help with the language. "To get anything important done requires fluency in Japanese," he says.

OTHER OPPORTUNITIES

Japan's changing economic, demographic and political environment offers some interesting opportunities. While a detailed treatment of these investments is outside the scope of this book, they merit a brief description.

Commercial property

Despite a brief rebound in 2007/8, commercial real estate has been a poor investment over the last two decades. While prices of commercial and residential land rose from 1978 to 1991, the value of residential land has declined less than commercial land since the 1991 peak. Over the past 20 years, office rents in Tokyo, Osaka and Nagoya have been flat or have declined.[1] At the end of January 2010, the office vacancy rate in central Tokyo was over 8%, while Osaka topped 10% and Nagoya exceeded 12%.[2]

Office and commercial space is usually sold on an en bloc (whole building) or multi-floor basis, putting it beyond the reach of most individual investors. "Pencil buildings," which are tall, thin structures erected on small plots of land, may be worth investigating. Typically purchased in a cash deal for as little as ¥100 million, these commercial buildings can offer attractive yields.

Farmland

Japan's farmers are old and their numbers are shrinking fast. Of the 3.1 million people actively involved in farming in 2007, 59% were 65 or older and the population of farm households in rural areas dropped from 11.6 million people in 1997 to 7.6 million in 2007.[3] As farmers retire and die, and their children take jobs in Japan's cities, agriculture is no longer the primary economic driver in many rural areas.[4]

While the farming population declines, the amount of abandoned farmland is increasing. In 2005, 390,000 hectares of farmland—almost twice the area of metropolitan Tokyo—had been abandoned, up from 240,000 hectares in 1995.[5]

At 1.6 hectares, the average Japanese farm is 1/20 the size of a German farm and less than 1% of an American farm.[6] Recently, agricultural laws have been amended to allow companies to buy farmland under certain conditions, increase the maximum stake corporations can take in a farm and raise the maximum term for corporate leases of farmland.

Despite these changes, reforming Japan's agricultural sector will not be easy. Farms and farmers occupy a special place in the national psyche, and there are powerful government, industry and community groups with an interest in maintaining the present system. This includes rural committees that must approve purchases of farmland by outsiders.

Homes for the elderly

With nearly one-third of the population projected to be over 65 by 2030, Japan faces a shortage of homes for the elderly.

Private assisted living facilities are operated by companies such as Nichii Gakkan (www.nichiigakkan.co.jp, Japanese only) and Benesse (www.benesse.co.jp). There are also public and semipublic homes, many of which are spartan and located in suburban and rural areas where costs are lower. Small, low-cost facilities often operate without a license.[7]

In 2009, 400,000 people were waiting for places in long-term care facilities covered by the nursing care insurance program.[8] By 2025, 5.2 million people, nearly half of whom will be bedridden, will need long-term care.[9] The shortage of nursing home space results in elderly people staying in hospitals, which are not equipped to meet their needs. In one study, people over 65 comprised nearly half of all hospital patients and more than 40% remained in the hospital for six months or longer.[10]

In recent years, Japan's nursing homes have been embroiled in scandals involving overbilling, misrepresenting staff numbers,[11] mistreating residents and failing to meet safety standards.[12] The long-term care industry suffers from labor shortages, exacerbated by low wages, shift work and poor working conditions.

Love hotels

Japan has tens of thousands of love hotels, where amorous couples can escape for a few hours of privacy. Love hotels, which are also known as leisure hotels, are an accepted part of life in a nation where homes are small and many people live with their parents into middle age.[13]

Love hotels are outside the mainstream hospitality industry and operators often have difficulty arranging financing. The industry is fragmented, with many operators owning only a handful of hotels.[14]

Love hotels have two rates: A "rest" price of around ¥3,000 per hour and an overnight rate that can range from ¥6,000 to ¥30,000. This pricing structure allows well-managed properties to rent a room three times a day and generate revenues of ¥400,000 to ¥800,000 per month, per room.[15] The need for discretion means the hotels operate on a cash basis.

The recession-proof nature of this business has attracted interest from investors. Initia Star Securities (www.initia-star.com, Japanese only) operates a love hotel mutual fund, while Japan Leisure Hotels (www.japanleisurehotels.com) is a closed-end investment company that is traded on the London Stock Exchange's AIM market.

Low-cost housing

The economic downturn that began in 2008 has created demand for inexpensive housing for students, "freeters" and unemployed people who cannot afford a conventional apartment. Some take refuge in all-night Internet cafes, known as *manga kissa*. Capsule hotels, which were originally intended for salarymen who missed the last train home, are being converted into low-cost residences. Other people rent space in "closet houses," in what are effectively enclosed bunk beds. Costing as little as ¥1,500 a night or ¥18,000 per month, these premises include storage lockers and shared bathrooms and kitchens.[16] Some small investors are buying foreclosed homes and converting them into closet houses.

Rental accommodation for expatriates

Unlike in many countries, where locals and foreigners live side-by-side, there is little crossover between the expatriate* and domestic markets in Japan. The Western-style bathrooms, gourmet kitchens and wall-to-wall carpets preferred by expats do not appeal to most Japanese renters.

*"Expatriate" refers here to an employee who has been dispatched to Japan (often with family in tow), receives a housing allowance and lives in a Western-style home. This is in contrast to foreign nationals who have been hired on local terms and pay their own housing and living expenses. Both are foreigners, but they are distinct markets.

The September 2008 collapse of Lehman Brothers, which had a large expat presence in Tokyo, and the subsequent economic downturn, left an oversupply of centrally located apartments catering to the tastes (and budgets) of Western executives. With a shrinking pool of expatriate families, some owners are converting homes in Roppongi and Azabu into luxury shared accommodation for single foreigners.[17] Many people find these arrangements preferable to renting a small, one-room apartment and similar projects are being developed in other parts of Tokyo.

Stocks and mutual funds

If you would prefer not buy physical property, there are several other ways to gain exposure to the Japanese real estate market. You can:

- Buy shares in home builders such as Daiwa House (www. daiwahouse.co.jp), Misawa Homes (www.misawa.co.jp), Sekisui House (www.sekisuihouse.co.jp) or Sumitomo Forestry (http://sfc.jp).

- Purchase shares in developers such as Mitsubishi Estate (www. mec.co.jp), Mitsui Fudosan (www.mitsuifudosan.co.jp), NTT Urban Development (www.nttud.co.jp) or Sumitomo Realty & Development (www.sumitomo-rd.co.jp).

- Buy shares in asset management companies such as Star Mica (www.starmica.co.jp) or Secured Capital Japan (www.securedcapital.co.jp).

- Invest in a J-REIT (Japanese real estate investment trust). See the Association for Real Estate Securitization Website (www.ares.or.jp) for more information.

- Invest in a mutual fund, such as the Fidelity International Real Estate Fund (www.fidelity.com) or the ING International Real Estate Fund (www.ingfunds.com).

RESOURCES

USEFUL INFORMATION

This chapter provides a list of resources that can help you with a wide range of issues when buying property or living in Japan. Websites are provided for further research, which unless otherwise noted are in English. Most of these resources are free of charge. Since organizations often restructure their Websites, the addresses given are generally for the main page, which may be in Japanese with an English (or "Global") option.

Groups representing Japan's real estate and construction industries are included to provide statistics and background information, as well as some non-Japanese design and construction Websites. These listings are not exhaustive—searching the Internet is a good place to start when investigating how to negotiate the Japanese real estate market.

Finally, Japan's governments supply information on a variety of topics. See "Government: Municipal," "Government: National" and "Government: Prefectural" below.

Antiquities

The Agency for Cultural Affairs is responsible for antiquities and archeological relics (www.bunka.go.jp). Your local city or ward office has maps showing the location of archeological sites in their administrative area.

Appraisal services

Many English-speaking real estate appraisers work in Japan and most have a Website. Prices range from ¥20,000 for a one-page form letter appraisal for a vacant lot to more than ¥200,000 for a detailed report covering the rental of a building.

The Japanese Association of Real Estate Appraisal has a Website with English-language papers on a range of topics (www.fudousan-kanteishi.or.jp). The Japanese section includes links to prefectural appraisal associations and individual appraisers.

The Tokyo Association of Real Estate Appraisers' Website includes commentary on Tokyo's residential housing market (www.tokyo-kanteishi.or.jp). The Japanese section includes a list of appraisers.

Architects and designers

ArchDaily features the work of architects from around the world, with many examples from Japan (www.archdaily.com).

Japan has more than 500,000 architects and building engineers (*kenchikushi*), about 35,000 of whom are members of the Architectural Institute of Japan (www.aij.or.jp).

The Japan Architectural Education and Information Center conducts examinations for kenchikushi and supervises their training (www.jaeic.or.jp). The center also certifies interior planners, whose services include interior design and architecture, as well as supervising construction work inside a building. The center's Website includes a detailed explanation of how architects are certified and the services that various grades of architects are permitted to provide. English-language translations of the Kenchikushi Act for Architects & Building Engineers (Act No. 202 of 1950) can be purchased on the center's Website, which includes the Ministry of Land, Infrastructure, Transport and Tourism's guidelines for designing homes for the elderly (Japanese only).

The Japan Federation of Architects & Building Engineers Association's Website includes links to each prefecture's architectural association (www.kenchikushikai.or.jp, Japanese only). The site can help you find an architect and includes information about the licensing and certification of architects.

The Website of the Japan Federation of Interior Planners' Association (www.jipa-official.org, Japanese only) has links to regional associations, including Tokyo (www.jipat.gr.jp), Chugoku (http://cipa21.com), Chubu (www.chubu-ip.com), Hokkaido (www.hipa.biz), Kansai (www.jipa.net/kipa) and Shizuoka (http://ipas2006.hp.infoseek.co.jp). Each regional Website includes links to member companies. All sites, except for Tokyo, are only in Japanese.

The Japan Institute of Architects describes itself as "Japan's only professional organization of architects" (www.jia.or.jp). Some 4,700 practitioners throughout Japan belong to the institute, which is affiliated with the International Union of Architects. The institute's Website includes information about certification and professional development and has a search function for architects.

The Japan Interior Designers' Association (www.jid.or.jp) divides Japan into four regions: Chubu (www.jid-chubu.org), Kansai (www.jid-kansai.jp), Kanto (http://jid-kanto.org) and Kyushu (www.jid-kyusyu.org). The regional chapters' Websites are only in Japanese and include links to members.

The Japan Interior Industry Association represents companies supplying the decoration and construction industries (www.interior.or.jp, Japanese only). The association's Website includes links to member companies, design schools and related organizations.

The Royal Institute of British Architects (www.architecture.com) and the American Institute of Architects (www.aia.org) offer booklets on how to hire and work with an architect. The American Institute of Architects has a chapter in Japan (http://aiajapan.org).

The World Architects' Website (www.world-architects.com) includes a directory of Japanese architects, complete with photographs (www.japan-architects.com).

Build it yourself

Arudou Debito (formerly David Aldwinckle), a naturalized Japanese citizen and associate professor at a Hokkaido university, bought land and built a house in the countryside in 1997 (www.debito.org/residentspage.html#HOUSEBUILDING).

FreeGreen (www.freegreen.com), Hometta (www.hometta.com) and Houseplans (www.houseplans.com) sell professionally designed building plans.

The U.K.-based National Self Build Association published a report called Selfbuild as a volume housing solution that examines trends, developments and the advantages of building your own home (www.nasba.org.uk).

Several organizations in the United States offer courses for people interested in learning to build their own home: the Shelter Institute (www.shelterinstitute.com), Rocky Mountain Workshops (www.rockymountainworkshops.com) and the Yestermorrow Design/Build School (www.yestermorrow.org).

Consumer protection

The Center for Housing Renovation and Dispute Settlement Support funds local bar associations that offer a channel for resolving housing-related disputes (www.chord.or.jp). The center also gathers information and provides Japanese-language telephone counseling on housing-related issues.

The National Association for Real Estate Transaction Guaranty (NARETG) settles disputes in property transactions handled by agents who are members of the National Federation of Real Estate Transaction Associations (www.zentaku.or.jp, Japanese only). The NARETG ensures a buyer's "earnest money" (deposit) is refunded if a transaction becomes invalid. If a consumer buys a property from a member agent and makes a deposit of more than 10% of the property's value or more than ¥10 million, the local NARETG office holds the deposit on behalf of the seller until the transaction is successfully completed.

The National Consumer Affairs Center of Japan provides consumer counseling, conducts research, collects data and publishes an English-language newsletter every two months (www.kokusen.go.jp).

The Organization for Housing Warranty is the largest supplier of home warranties in Japan, providing coverage for new structures, extensions and additions (www.how.or.jp, Japanese only). Home warranties are nontransferable, but the organization sells warranties on used homes as well as completion warranties that protect a buyer if a contractor becomes insolvent. For a detailed explanation of Japan's home warranties, see www.ihhwc.jp/sessions/World_Research.pdf.

Earthquakes

The Japan Building Disaster Prevention Association offers information for professionals and homeowners about evaluating and retrofitting buildings (www.kenchiku-bosai.or.jp).

The Japan Map Center sells maps showing the active faults in Japan's urban areas, as well as places likely to be affected by liquefaction in an earthquake (www.jmc.or.jp).

The Tokyo Metropolitan Government has prepared a bilingual earthquake survival guide (www.seikatubunka.metro.tokyo.jp/index3files/survivalmanual.pdf).

The United States Geological Survey has general background on earthquakes (http://earthquake.usgs.gov).

The elderly

The Foundation for Senior Citizens' Housing researches and certifies housing for the elderly, promotes universal design and publishes reports, books and design manuals (www.koujuuzai.or.jp, Japanese only).

Energy

The Energy Conservation Center, Japan, provides information about national energy policies, government subsidies, tax incentives and related resources for businesses and individuals (www.eccj.or.jp). It also has a database of energy-saving equipment.

For information about solar power subsidies and incentives, see your prefectural or local government office and the Japan Photovoltaic Expansion Center (www.j-pec.or.jp, Japanese only).

The Japan Photovoltaic Energy Association has case studies, background information and checklists for people thinking of installing a residential solar power system (www.jpea.gr.jp, Japanese only).

Japan's largest manufacturers of solar panels are Kyocera Corp. (www.kyocera.co.jp), Mitsubishi Electric Corp. (http://mitsubishielectric.co.jp), Sanyo Electric Co. (http://jp.sanyo.com) and Sharp Corp. (www.sharp.co.jp). Residential solar panels are sold through electrical appliance dealers, building equipment suppliers and sales agents.

Environmental

The Asbestos Center provides information and support about asbestos-related issues (http://asbestos-center.jp). The center was involved in the production of two Japanese-language books: *Why Did the Asbestos Disaster Spread?* (Nippon-Hyoron-Sha Co., 2009, www.nippyo.co.jp, ISBN: 978-4-535-58487-7), which traces the history of asbestos in Japan, and *Diagnosing the Asbestos Hazard* (Asahi Shimbun, 2005, www.asahi.com, ISBN: 978-4-022-50081-6), an illustrated guide to identifying asbestos in buildings. Both publishers' Websites are in Japanese.

The Building Center of Japan has information about the standards for building materials as they relate to sick house syndrome and sells translations of the Building Standard Law and summaries of the Housing Quality Assurance Act and Japan Housing Performance Indication Standards (www.bcj.or.jp).

The Comprehensive Assessment System for Building Environmental Efficiency (CASBEE) is a series of assessment tools that rate a building's environmental performance and load on the external environment (www.ibec.or.jp/CASBEE). CASBEE is applicable to commercial and residential buildings and detached homes and includes tools for design and renovation projects as well as English-language checklists.

The Geo-Environmental Protection Center of Japan has a list of companies providing soil testing and remediation services (www.gepc.or.jp).

The United States Environmental Protection Agency has information about indoor air quality as well as volatile organic compounds (www.epa.gov).

Floods and landslides

The Foundation of River & Basin Integrated Communications has information about flood hazards (www.river.or.jp/hazard/link/search.html, Japanese only).

The Japan Landslide Society researches landslides and their prevention (www.landslide-soc.org).

The Japan Map Center (www.jmc.or.jp) sells maps showing areas likely to be affected by flooding.

Finance

Lenders

The following organizations offer housing loans. This is not an exhaustive list, as it excludes all but one of Japan's 108 regional banks. These lenders may be worth contacting if you are buying property in their operating area.

With the exception of the foreign banks, Shinsei Bank and Suruga Bank, the mortgage information on the lenders' Websites is in Japanese. However, many lenders have English-language investor relations materials, such as fact books and annual reports, on their Websites.

City banks

Bank of Tokyo-Mitsubishi UFJ (www.bk.mufg.jp)
Mizuho Bank (www.mizuhobank.co.jp)
Resona Bank (www.resona-gr.co.jp/resonabank)
Sumitomo Mitsui Banking Corp. (www.smbc.co.jp)

Foreign banks

Commonwealth Bank of Australia (www.commbank.co.jp)
The Hongkong and Shanghai Banking Corp. (www.hsbc.co.jp)
National Australia Bank (www.nabasia.co.jp)

Trust banks

Chuo Mitsui Trust and Banking Co. (www.chuomitsui.jp)
Mitsubishi UFJ Trust and Banking Corp. (www.tr.mufg.jp)
Mizuho Trust Bank (www.mizuho-tb.co.jp)
Sumitomo Trust & Banking Co. (www.sumitomotrust.co.jp)

Others

Aeon Bank (www.aeonbank.co.jp)
Aozora Bank (www.aozorabank.co.jp)
ORIX Trust and Banking Corp. (http://trust.orix.co.jp)
SBI Mortgage Co. (www.sbi-mortgage.co.jp)
Shinsei Bank (www.shinseibank.com)
Sony Bank (http://sonybank.net)
Suruga Bank (www.surugabank.co.jp)
Tokyo Star Bank (www.tokyostarbank.co.jp)

Other resources

Aggregators and brokers

The E-LOAN Website aggregates mortgage information from more than 60 lenders (www.eloan.co.jp, Japanese only).

IFG Asia Mortgages provides English-language mortgage broking services for people wishing to buy property in Japan (www.ifgasiamortgages.com).

The Housing Loan Progress Association (www.hlpa.or.jp, Japanese only) operates a separate Website that lets you search for a mortgage adviser by geographical area, expertise and professional qualifications (www.loan-adviser.jp, Japanese only).

Credit bureaus

The Personal Credit Information Center (www.zenginkyo.or.jp)

The Credit Information Center (www.cic.co.jp)

The Japan Credit Information Reference Center (www.jicc.co.jp)

The Japan Consumer Credit Industry Association (www.j-credit.or.jp, Japanese only)

The Japanese Bankers Association

The Japanese Bankers Association provides background on Japan's banking laws and regulations (www.zenginkyo.or.jp). The association's site includes a list of members, with links to many of Japan's banks and information about Japan's credit bureaus.

Reverse mortgages

The U.S.-based National Reverse Mortgage Lenders Association operates a Website with calculators, resources and background information about reverse mortgages (www.reversemortgage.org).

Fire

The Tokyo Fire Department maintains a multilingual Website with a variety of fire- and safety-related information (www.tfd.metro.tokyo.jp). The department also operates the Life Safety Learning Center, which features a smoke-filled maze, simulations of earthquakes and rainstorms, first-aid and fire-prevention courses and information for children (www.tfd.metro.tokyo.jp/hp-hjbskan, Japanese only).

General housing information

The Building and Housing Center of Japan organizes fairs and other events to promote quality housing (http://bhcj.co.jp, Japanese only).

The Center for Better Living provides testing and certification for building components and systems, ranging from elevators and windows to kitchens and bathrooms (www.cbl.or.jp). Products bearing the BL logo are covered by a warranty of between two and 10 years. BL certification also includes product liability insurance, which covers accidents causing injury, death or property damage due to flaws or defects in an item's design, manufacture or installation.

The Condominium Management Center offers information about maintaining and managing condominiums, as well as training and certification programs (www.mankan.or.jp, Japanese only).

The Housing Information Center offers a searchable database of specialist contractors and material suppliers (www.hic.or.jp, Japanese only).

The Housing Information Council features consumer-oriented information about laws, antiseismic treatments, reform, security, sick building syndrome, sustainability and more (www.sumai-info.jp, Japanese only).

The Japan Federation of Housing Organizations has information about environmentally friendly designs, urban planning, financing and more (www.judanren.or.jp).

Government: Municipal
Tokyo

The Tokyo Metropolitan Government's Website includes a guide for foreign residents as well as information about public safety, transportation, healthcare, education, tourism and other topics (www.metro.tokyo.jp).

In addition to being the nation's capital and business hub, Tokyo has many parks and recreational facilities.

You can check the credentials of real estate companies against lists maintained by the Tokyo Metropolitan Government and the Ministry of Land, Infrastructure, Transport and Tourism (www.takken.metro.tokyo.jp, Japanese only).

Tokyo's 23 wards have Websites with English-language content ranging from brief summaries to monthly newsletters. Many sites include maps showing disaster evacuation routes, as well as seismic and flood hazards. Links to each of Tokyo's wards, cities and islands can be found at www.metro.tokyo.jp/ENGLISH/LINKS/links1.htm.

Other major cities

Chiba (www.city.chiba.jp)

Fukuoka (www.city.fukuoka.lg.jp)

Hiroshima (www.city.hiroshima.lg.jp)

Kawasaki (www.city.kawasaki.jp)

Kitakyushu (www.city.kitakyushu.jp)

Kobe (www.city.kobe.lg.jp)

Kyoto (www.city.kyoto.lg.jp)

Nagoya (www.city.nagoya.jp)

Nagasaki (www.city.nagasaki.nagasaki.jp)

Okayama (www.city.okayama.jp)

Osaka (www.city.osaka.lg.jp)

Sakai (www.city.sakai.lg.jp/index.html)

Sapporo (http://web.city.sapporo.jp)

Sendai (www.city.sendai.jp)

Yokohama (www.city.yokohama.jp)

Government: National

Land, real estate and related issues fall under the jurisdiction of many agencies, ministries and bureaus. Here are some of the key ones.

The Agency for Cultural Affairs is responsible for antiquities and archeological relics (www.bunka.go.jp).

Although, technically, it is not a government agency, the Bank of Japan sets and implements the nation's monetary policy and publishes the quarterly *tankan* survey of business trends (www.boj.or.jp).

The Cabinet Office produces research reports on social, business and economic topics (www.cao.go.jp).

The Consumer Affairs Agency protects consumers and addresses disputes from the perspective of individuals (www.caa.go.jp). The agency's jurisdiction includes the Real Estate Transaction Act and the Money Lending Control Act.

The Financial Services Agency is responsible for the stability of Japan's financial system and protecting depositors, insurance policyholders and securities investors (www.fsa.go.jp). The agency's Website has lists of licensed banks, insurance companies and other providers of financial services, as well as English translations of finance laws.

The Geographical Survey Institute produces topographical, land use, coastal and hazard maps, which show areas likely to be affected by floods, earthquakes, liquefaction, lava flows and tsunamis (www.gsi.go.jp). The institute's maps and aerial photographs can be purchased from the Japan Map Center (www.jmc.or.jp).

The Headquarters for Earthquake Research Promotion provides information about current seismic activity, threat assessments, maps and other data (www.jishin.go.jp).

The Japan Housing Finance Agency purchases long-term, fixed-rate loans from private financial institutions for securitization (www.jhf.go.jp). The agency's main product, Flat 35, is a fixed-rate housing loan with a maximum term of 35 years that is widely available from lenders throughout Japan. The agency also offers Flat 50, a 50-year version of Flat 35.

The Japan Meteorological Agency provides information about weather and operates an earthquake early-warning system (www.jma.go.jp). The agency's Website includes detailed information about local seismic activity, tsunami warnings and an explanation of the JMA Seismic Intensity Scale.

The Japan Seismic Hazard Information Station maintains a map showing the nation's earthquake hotspots and an earthquake-probability calculator (www.j-shis.bosai.go.jp, Japanese only).

The Justice Department's Legal Affairs Bureau explains how to register real estate electronically and lists office locations nationwide (http://houmukyoku.moj.go.jp, Japanese only).

The Ministry of Agriculture, Forestry and Fisheries administers farmland and forests and promotes the development of rural areas (www.maff.go.jp).

The Ministry of the Environment handles issues relating to agrichemicals, asbestos, contaminated soil and polychlorinated biphenyls (PCBs). The MoE has background information, statistics and English translations of environmental laws on its Website (www.env.go.jp), as well as links to asbestos-related topics.

Each December, the Ministry of Finance produces a report summarizing the changes to the tax system to be implemented in the following fiscal year (www.mof.go.jp). The ministry's Website includes an excerpt from the Income Tax Act as it relates to nonresidents and foreign corporations, and the Comprehensive Handbook of Japanese Taxes 2006.

The Ministry of Health, Labour and Welfare is involved in environmental, aging and pension issues (www.mhlw.go.jp).

Japanese Law Translation, operated by the Ministry of Justice, has English versions of over 180 Japanese laws, keyword search capabilities and translations of more than 3,700 legal terms (www.japaneselawtranslation.go.jp).

The Ministry of Land, Infrastructure, Transport and Tourism (MLIT) features the following information on its Website (http://tochi.mlit.go.jp):

- The quarterly *Land Price Look Report* shows price trends in 65 districts in Tokyo, 39 in Osaka, 14 in Nagoya and 32 in regional urban centers. The report also looks at 42 residential and 108 commercial areas.

- An interactive section provides historical sales data from the third quarter of fiscal 2005 for residential, commercial and industrial property, as well as for farmland and forests throughout Japan (www.land.mlit.go.jp/webland). The site, which is updated quarterly, includes detailed English-language maps.

- The *Monthly Marketing Report on Lands* summarizes sales and rental data and trends for commercial and residential property as well as J-REITs (Japanese real estate investment trusts).

- The annual *Summary of White Paper on Land* provides an overview of land use and demand trends, real estate industry and policy initiatives and price and transaction data. This is a helpful starting point for learning about Japanese real estate.

- An explanation of the taxes on the acquisition, possession and transfer of land.

- Background about asbestos (www.mlit.go.jp/kisha/kisha06/ 07/071213_.html, Japanese only), seismic preparedness and other building issues (most of which is in Japanese).

- Flood-control measures for Tokyo's Arakawa River.

MLIT also operates Anshin Chintai (Trusted Renting Net), a multilingual Website that helps the elderly, foreigners, disabled people and families with children find rental accommodations (www. anshin-chintai.jp).

MLIT and the Japan International Cooperation Agency published *Urban Planning System in Japan*, a 70-page booklet that explains the intricacies of Japan's urban planning processes (http:// lvzopac.jica.go.jp).

The National Diet Library has statistics and information about Japan (www.ndl.go.jp).

The National Institute of Population and Social Security Research publishes data and research in English, Chinese and Korean (www.ipss.go.jp).

The National Research Institute for Earth Science and Disaster Prevention maintains detailed, nationwide maps of areas prone to landslides (http://lsweb1.ess.bosai.go.jp) and floods (http://engan.bosai.go.jp, Japanese only).

The National Tax Agency publishes an annual income tax guide for foreigners that includes a directory of tax offices and an explanation of Japan's tax system (www.nta.go.jp).

NHK, Japan's national broadcaster, maintains a Website with news in text, podcast and video formats (www.nhk.or.jp). Programming is available in Japanese, English and 17 other languages. NHK's domestic radio and television channels are required by law to broadcast warnings about floods, typhoons, tsunamis and earthquakes.

The Statistics Bureau, which is part of the Ministry of Internal Affairs and Communications, compiles data on life in Japan (www.stat.go.jp). The bureau produces regular surveys, monthly statistical reports, the detailed *Japan Statistical Yearbook* and a more user-friendly annual *Statistical Handbook of Japan*. The bureau also conducts a census every five years, most recently in 2005.

The Supreme Court of Japan explains Japan's legal system, the structure of the nation's courts and the procedures for criminal and civil cases (www.courts.go.jp).

Government: Prefectural

Japan's 47 prefectures have Websites that include content in English and other languages. Links to the Websites can be found at www.japan-guide.com/list/e1002.html.

The Council of Local Authorities for International Relations promotes local-level internationalization in Japan and maintains a Website that explains the function and structure of Japan's prefectural governments (www.clair.or.jp).

Home builders

Domestic

Content on these Websites is primarily in Japanese.

Asahi Kasei Homes (www.asahi-kasei.co.jp)

Daiwa House (www.daiwahouse.co.jp)

Higashi Nihon House (www.higashinihon.co.jp)

Hosoda (www.hosoda.co.jp)

Misawa Homes (www.misawa.co.jp)

Mitsubishi Estate Home (www.mitsubishi-home.com)

Mitsui Home (www.mitsuihome.co.jp)

PanaHome (www.panahome.jp)

Sanyo Home (www.sanyohomes.co.jp)

Shin-Nihon Tatemono (www.kksnt.co.jp)

Sekisui Heim (www.sekisuiheim.com)

Sekisui House (www.sekisuihouse.co.jp)

Selco Home (http://selcohome.jp)

Sumitomo Forestry (http://sfc.jp)

Sumitomo Realty & Development (www.sumitomo-rd.co.jp)

SxL (www.sxl.co.jp)

Tokyu Homes (www.tokyu-homes.co.jp)

Toyota Home (www.toyotahome.co.jp)

Log houses

In Japan, a log house refers to an imported wooden home. This can include post-and-beam homes as well as houses made from stacked logs, like a traditional log cabin.

Two of the largest log house companies are Lindal Cedar Homes (www.lindaljapan.com, Japanese only, but www.lindal.com has information in English) and Sweden House (www.swedenhouse. co.jp, Japanese only). There are numerous smaller companies including Akane Planning (www.akane-plan.co.jp), Bess (www.bess.jp, Japanese only) and Eastloghouse (www.eastloghouse. jp, Japanese only), that import log houses.

Industry associations

The Imported House Industries Organization has a list of member companies and general information about imported homes in Japan (www.ihio.or.jp, Japanese only).

The Japan Prefabricated Construction Suppliers & Manufacturers Association explains how prefab homes are designed and built and offers tips about care and maintenance (www.purekyo.or.jp, Japanese only).

The Japan Association of Home Suppliers represents builders and related companies (www.nichijukyo.or.jp, Japanese only).

The Log Home Builders Association of North America offers classes and information for people interested in building a log home (www.loghomebuilders.org).

The Real Estate Companies Association of Japan represents builders and related companies (www.fdk.or.jp).

Insurance

The Non-Life Insurance Rating Organization of Japan has an exhaustive explanation of earthquake insurance in Japan (www.nliro.or.jp). For a more reader-friendly summary, see the annual reports of the Japan Earthquake Reinsurance Company (www.nihonjishin.co.jp) or the General Insurance Association of Japan (www.sonpo.or.jp). The GIAJ site includes a fact book, a members list and other data about the non-life insurance market.

The Foreign Non-Life Insurance Association of Japan maintains a list of international companies licensed to provide non-life insurance in Japan (www.fnlia.gr.jp).

The Independent Insurance Agents of Japan has a consumer-oriented explanation of Japan's non-life insurance sector, including the structure of fire insurance policies (www.nihondaikyo.or.jp, Japanese only).

International brands

Many leading international furniture, accessory and equipment brands are represented in Japan through dealers or dedicated showrooms. Numerous design-oriented complexes, such as Ozone (www.ozone.co.jp) and the Tokyo Design Center (www.design-center.co.jp), feature local and international brands.

International brands available in Japan		
Brand	**Website**	**Product**
Armstrong	www.armstrong.co.jp	Floor and ceiling coverings
Bang & Olufsen	www.bang-olufsen.com	Audiovisual equipment
Cassina	www.cassina-ixc.com	Le Corbusier and Frank Lloyd Wright furniture
Conran	www.conran.ne.jp	Furnishings
Crestron	http://crestronjapan.com	Lighting and home automation systems
Duravit	www.duravit.com	Sanitaryware
Giorgio Armani	www.giorgioarmanistores.com	Furniture and accessories
Gaggenau	www.gaggenau.com	Kitchens and appliances
Hansgrohe	www.hansgrohe.co.jp	Plumbing
Herman Miller	www.hermanmiller.co.jp	Eames and Aeron chairs
Hunter Douglas	www.hunterdouglas.jp	Window coverings
Ikea	www.ikea.co.jp	Furniture and accessories
Lutron	http://asia.lutron.com	Lighting and home automation systems
Miele	www.miele.com	Appliances
Philippe Stark	www.starck.com	Furniture and accessories
Poggen Pohl	www.poggenpohl.com	Kitchens and appliances
Ralph Lauren	http://ralphlauren.jp	Furniture and accessories
Snaidero	www.snaidero.com	Kitchens
Valcucine	www.valcucine.it	Kitchens

J-REITs

The Association for Real Estate Securitization Website summarizes the J-REITs (Japanese real estate investment trusts) listed on Japanese stock exchanges (www.ares.or.jp). The site includes information about the assets, performance and investor base of each J-REIT.

Law

The Japan Commercial Arbitration Association provides dispute resolution services, including mediation and arbitration, in English and Japanese under the United Nations Commission on International Trade Law (UNCITRAL) rules (www.jcaa.or.jp).

The Japan Federation of Bar Associations' Website has information about fee-based legal counseling for foreigners from local bar associations throughout Japan (www.nichibenren.or.jp). The federation also operates the Japan Legal Support Center telephone hotline (0570-07-8374).

Judicial scriveners (*shiho-shoshi*) handle the transfer of land and building titles in Japan. These specialist lawyers can also handle other, minor legal matters. The English-language section of the Japan Federation of Shiho-Shoshi Lawyers Associations' Website explains the services offered by shiho-shoshi (www.shiho-shoshi.or.jp). The Japanese portion includes a nationwide directory of shiho-shoshi.

The National Center for the Elimination of Boryokudan provides information about the yakuza and how to deal with them (www1a.biglobe.ne.jp/boutsui/index2.htm, Japanese only).

The University of California Hastings College of the Law Library maintains a comprehensive list of Japanese legal resources (http://library.uchastings.edu/library/foreign-and-international-research/japaneselaw.html).

Media

Japan-based media

The *ACCJ Journal* is a free online monthly magazine published by the American Chamber of Commerce in Japan (www.accj.or.jp). The magazine occasionally publishes articles about real estate–related topics and features ads from banks and other businesses targeting foreigners.

The *Asahi Shimbun*, a leading Japanese daily, publishes an English-language edition in conjunction with the *International Herald Tribune* and *New York Times* (www.asahi.com/english). The English edition is available free on the company's Website, with some archive access.

The *Daily Yomiuri* is the English edition of the country's largest circulation daily newspaper, the *Yomiuri Shimbun* (www.yomiuri.co.jp/dy). News stories and limited archive access are available free on the paper's Website.

Japan Inc is a quarterly business magazine matched with blogs and online newsletters and a searchable archive (www.japaninc.com). An RSS feed lets you subscribe to the magazine.

The Japan Times is Japan's leading English newspaper (www.
japantimes.co.jp). Reading the paper and searching its archives are
free online. An RSS feed is available.

Japan Today (www.japantoday.com) is an online newspaper
that includes Japan-focused stories from wire services such as
Kyodo News (http://home.kyodo.co.jp) and the Associated Press
(www.ap.org) that are only available to subscribers, stories from
magazines like *Metropolis* (http://metropolis.co.jp) and original
content. An RSS feed and forums are available.

The Mainichi Daily News is the English edition of the *Mainichi Shimbun* (http://mdn.mainichi.jp). News stories, limited archive access
and an RSS feed are available on the paper's Website.

Nikkei Inc. is Japan's preeminent source of business news
(www.nni.nikkei.co.jp). Nikkei publishes several Japanese newspa-
pers and the English business newspaper *Nikkei Weekly*. A limited
amount of news is available free on the company's Website. A paid
subscription provides access to more information and Nikkei's archives. The company also publishes the Nikkei Real Estate Market
Report (http://realestate.nikkeibp.co.jp), an online, fee-based news
service.

Recruit Co. publishes the Japanese-language housing magazine
Suumo (www.suumo.jp).

Shinkenchiku-sha Co. publishes books and magazines in Japanese
and English about design and architecture (www.shinkenchiku.net).

The Real Estate Economic Institute produces a weekly English-
language summary of real estate news (www.fudousankeizai.co.jp).
The summary is searchable and available by subscription.

The housing blog Cat Foreheads & Rabbit Hutches covers stories from
the Japanese-language media (http://catforehead.wordpress.com).

International media

While not as frequent or extensive as the coverage from domestic
news sources, the following outlets provide useful information on
business and social topics.

Bloomberg is a global financial wire service (www.bloomberg.com).
News stories are free on the company's Website. Bloomberg is a
good source of business and economic data.

The Economist is a weekly publication covering general and business news (www.economist.com). Large sections of *The Economist*'s content are free, although full archive access requires a subscription. RSS feeds are available.

The Financial Times is a London-based, global business newspaper (www.ft.com). On Saturdays, it includes a global real estate section called House & Home. Much of the paper and its archives are free or free with registration. RSS feeds are available.

The New York Times (www.nytimes.com) and its global edition, the *International Herald Tribune* (www.iht.com), cover business and general events in Japan. Both papers report on residential real estate around the world.

Reuters is a global wire service that covers general and business news (www.reuters.com). News stories and archived material are free on the company's Website, which includes RSS feeds for a variety of subjects. Reuters also operates www.reutersrealestate.com, which offers real estate news on a free and subscription basis.

The Wall Street Journal is a U.S.-based, global business newspaper (www.wsj.com). Sections of the newspaper and its archive are free, while full access requires a subscription. RSS feeds are available.

Niseko

Aero Asahi (www.aeroasahi.co.jp) offers helicopter transfers from Sapporo's New Chitose Airport (www.new-chitose-airport.jp) to Niseko. New Chitose Airport is the nearest international airport to the resort area.

Hokkaido Aviation (www.hokkaido-koku.co.jp) provides helicopter transfers to Niseko from Sapporo's Okadama Airport (www.okadama-airport.co.jp).

Hokkaido Railway, also known as JR Hokkaido, provides train services throughout Hokkaido, including services from Sapporo's New Chitose Airport to Niseko (www.jrhokkaido.co.jp).

The Hokkaido Tracks Group comprises a travel agency, Hokkaido Tracks Holidays; a property developer, Hokkaido Tracks Resort Properties; and a property management company, Hokkaido Tracks Management (http://hokkaidotracks.com).

The Kutchannel is an online forum covering events in the Kutchan, Hirafu and Niseko areas (http://kutchannel.net). The site includes news, event listings, classified ads and more.

The official Website of Kutchan Town provides information about daily life in English and Japanese (www.town.kutchan.hokkaido.jp).

Australian-headquartered LJ Hooker sells residential property and vacant land in Niseko (www.ljhookerniseko.com).

Niseko Consulting offers property for sale and rent, as well as real estate consulting services (www.nisekoconsulting.com). The Website includes information about building regulations in the Niseko area.

Niseko Izumikyo sells property and land in the Niseko area (www.izumikyo.co.jp).

The Niseko Promotion Board offers information about a variety of topics in Chinese, English, Japanese and Korean (www.nisekotourism.com).

Niseko Property sells residential and commercial property as well as vacant land (www.nisekoproperty.com).

Niseko Resort Design & Construction designs and builds chalets, chateaus and condominiums and provides renovation and property management services (http://nisekordc.com). The company's site includes information about building in an alpine environment.

Nuclear power

The Federation of Electric Power Companies of Japan maintains a Website about Japan's nuclear power plants (www.japannuclear.com). Additional information is available from the World Nuclear Association (www.world-nuclear.org). Both sites promote the nuclear industry; for a less positive view, see the Citizens' Nuclear Information Center (http://cnic.jp).

Real estate agents

Japan has four main associations for the real estate industry. Each operates an Internet-based listing service and collaborates on a joint listing site, www.fudousan.or.jp, Japanese only.

The All Japan Real Estate Association (known in Japanese as Zennichi) is the parent organization of the Real Estate Guarantee Association, which resolves transaction-related complaints made against Zennichi members by other real estate agents (www.zennichi.or.jp). Zennichi operates an Internet-based listing service, Zennet (www.zennet.jp, Japanese only).

The Association of Real Estate Agents of Japan (Fudosan Ryutsu Keiei Kyokai, or FRK) (www.homenavi.or.jp/frk) operates the Homenavi (www.homenavi.or.jp) listing service and produces standard sales forms for its members' use. PDF versions of the forms, along with Japanese explanations, can be found on the FRK Website.

The National Federation of Real Estate Transaction Associations, known in Japanese as Zentakuren, claims 110,000 members or about 85% of the licensed real estate agents in Japan (www.zentaku.or.jp, Japanese only). Zentakuren operates the Hato Mark site (www.hatomarksite.com, Japanese only) listing service and the Zentaku Housing Loan Website (www.zentakuloan.co.jp, Japanese only), through which its members arrange housing loans for home buyers.

The Japan Association of Home Suppliers (www.nichijukyo. or.jp, Japanese only) represents developers, builders and related companies throughout Japan. The association's Website includes a list of members, links to related organizations and regular news updates.

The Tokyo Metropolitan Government operates a Website (www. takken.metro.tokyo.jp, Japanese only) where you can check the credentials of real estate companies against the lists maintained by the Tokyo Metropolitan Government and MLIT.

English-speaking agents

Akasaka Real Estate focuses on investment properties in the Tokyo area (www.akasakarealestate.com).

Asterisk Realty markets high-end property to international investors (www.asteriskrealty.jp).

Century 21 has franchises throughout Japan (www.century21japan. co.jp). The Website lists franchises with English-speaking staff.

Century 21 Smica Create offers residential sales and rental services in central Tokyo (www.century21-tokyo.com).

East Edge Partners provides asset advisory services including sourcing and brokerage, development and operation (www.ee-p.com).

Housing Japan handles residential sales and rentals in Tokyo and elsewhere (www.housingjapan.net).

Ken Corporation sells and rents property in Tokyo and Yokohama (www.kencorp.com).

Minato Asset Management provides sales, rental and investment services with an emphasis on vintage condominiums in central Tokyo (www.realestate-minato.com).

Mitsui Real Plan sells residential property, mainly in central Tokyo (www.realplan.jp).

Plaza Homes sells and rents commercial and residential property in Tokyo (www.realestate-tokyo.com).

Zee Brothers Homes provides residential sales and rental services in the Yokohama area (www.zbhomes.com).

Real estate listings

Individual buyers and sellers can access listings on several Internet sites, most of which include rentals and sales. There is considerable overlap in the listings on the mainstream sites. The primary difference between the sites is in how the listings are organized and whether a site specializes in a specific type of property or geographical area.

Mainstream listings

E-Life lists residential property, including vacant land, and new and used condominiums and houses and investment properties in Tokyo, Chiba, Kanagawa and Saitama (www.e-life.co.jp, Japanese only).

Fudousan lists all types of real estate and includes news, tips for buyers and legal information (www.fudousan.or.jp, Japanese only). Fudousan is jointly operated by Japan's four real estate industry associations: the All Japan Real Estate Association, the Association of Real Estate Agents of Japan, the National Federation of Real Estate Transaction Associations and the Japan Association of Home Suppliers. Each association operates a listing site, which is shown below.

Goo lists vacant land, new and used condominiums and houses and investment properties nationwide (http://house.goo.ne.jp, Japanese only).

The Hato Mark site is operated by the National Federation of Real Estate Transaction Associations (NFRETA) and lists property for sale and rent by NFRETA members in each of Japan's 47 prefectures. The NFRETA claims the Website is the largest association-run site in Japan (www.hatomarksite.com, Japanese only).

Homenavi is operated by the Association of Real Estate Agents (FRK) and lists vacant land as well as new and used houses and condominiums throughout Japan (www.homenavi.or.jp, Japanese only). Homenavi lists commercial and resort properties and includes a list of real estate agents and land brokers.

Home4U is operated by NTT Data and includes listings of vacant land as well as new and used houses and condominiums throughout Japan (http://home4u.jp, Japanese only). The site includes information about property managers and custom home builders.

Home's lists vacant land and new and used houses and condominiums throughout Japan (www.myhome-homes.jp, Japanese only). The site lets you sort property by features, such as corner lots, parking and barrier-free construction.

Microsoft's MSN Japan carries nationwide real estate listings, as well as information about reform, mortgages and related topics (http://jj.jp.msn.com, Japanese only). The site lists vacant land and new and used condominiums and houses.

Nichijukyo, which is operated by the Japan Association of Home Suppliers, lists land and residential, commercial and industrial property for sale and rent (www.nichijukyo.net, Japanese only).

Nomu is operated by Nomura Real Estate Urban Net (www.nomu. com, Japanese only). Nomu lists vacant land as well as new and used houses and condominiums, mainly in Tokyo and surrounding prefectures.

Suumo is a free magazine and nationwide listing site operated by Recruit that includes sales and rental information on new and used properties, as well as buying tips and background information (http://suumo.jp).

Yahoo! Japan's real estate site lists vacant land and new and used houses and condominiums nationwide (http://realestate.yahoo. co.jp, Japanese only). With registration, you can save searches, receive updates and access other services. The site also includes buying tips and real estate news.

Zennet is operated by the All Japan Real Estate Association and lists land as well as residential, commercial and industrial property for sale and rent (www.zennet.jp, Japanese only).

Specialist listings

Akasaka Real Estate has listings focusing on investment properties in the Tokyo area (www.akasakarealestate.com). The company's Website includes a database with detailed listings for houses, apartments, offices, land and rental property, historical data and analytical tools.

The Broadcast Information of Tri-set System is a searchable list of foreclosed properties for sale throughout Japan (http://bit.sikkou. jp, Japanese only). The site includes instructions for placing a bid, historical sales data, a glossary and other tools.

Foreclosed Japan offers English-language listings of foreclosed commercial and residential property, as well as vacant land, throughout Japan (http://foreclosedjapan.com). The site also features links to news stories about Japanese real estate gathered from a variety of sources.

Higashinihon Jutaku sells units in government-built condominiums (*kodan*) from the 1960s and 1970s (www.higashinihonjutaku.co.jp, Japanese only)

The Machiya Information Center has information about Kyoto's traditional *machiya* townhouses (www.kyomachiya.net, Japanese only). Information is available in English from the Kyoto Machiya Resource (www.kyotomachiya.com) and the Kyoto Center for Community Collaboration (http://kyoto-machisen.jp/fund).

The Real Estate Information Network System (REINS) is similar to the Multiple Listing Service (MLS) in the United States and Canada. Unlike MLS, however, access to REINS is limited to licensed real estate agents.

Riberesute is involved in several real estate businesses, including the purchase and liquidation of commercial and residential property (www.riberesute.co.jp, Japanese only). The company's site lists apartments and resort properties that include hot springs (*onsen*).

Reform (renovation)

The Housing Renovation Promoting Council's Website includes a series of standard home renovation contracts that can be downloaded as PDF files (www.j-reform.com, Japanese only). The council's members include industry associations, government bodies and product and service suppliers.

The home renovation business in Japan is represented by several industry groups. Jerco Reform is a nationwide organization with many of the largest hardware and equipment companies among its members. Jerco's Website includes a supplier search function and background information about planning renovation projects (www.jerco.or.jp, Japanese only).

The Remodeling Promotion Committee for Condominium Website features photos, floor plans and budgets for renovations intended to achieve a variety of goals, such as installing a home theater, and renovations to accommodate pets and the arrival and departure of children (www.repco.gr.jp, Japanese only).

Large home builders—including Misawa Homes, PanaHome, Sekusui Heim and Sumitomo Realty & Development—have subsidiaries and affiliates that provide reform services.

Rentals

Many real estate agents offer property management services, which allow them to earn commission on the sale and rental of property.

English translations of a regular and fixed-term residential lease are available from www.mlit.go.jp/jutakukentiku/house/torikumi/anshin/minkanguide/minkanguide3e.pdf.

The Property Manager Council provides training to property managers (www.chintaikanrishi.jp, Japanese only). The council's Website includes a search function as well as an ethics charter.

The Japan Property Management Association represents property managers and provides training, support and advice (www. jpm.jp). The association's Website includes links to property managers throughout Japan. The association also operates http:// welcome.jpm.jp, a multilingual Website designed to help its members rent properties to foreign tenants, and has produced a multilingual DVD to help foreigners rent property in Japan.[1]

Tokyo Room Finder has information about guest houses and other shared accommodation (www.tokyoroomfinder.com).

Research
Economic
Teikoku Databank provides corporate credit and market research services focusing on Japan. Highlights from the company's research, which includes monthly corporate confidence and bankruptcy statistics, are available in English from www.tdb.co.jp.

Tokyo Shoko Research sells credit information on Japanese businesses (www.tsr-net.co.jp).

General
Attractors Lab provides market research services about rents, vacancy rates, consumer preferences and market trends (www.a-lab.co.jp, Japanese only).

The Building Center of Japan describes itself as an incubator for new building technologies (www.bcj.or.jp). It publishes an annual yearbook, *A Quick Look at Housing in Japan*, that includes information about the nation's housing stock, housing policy and city planning. The center also sells translations of the Building Standard Law, the Housing Quality Assurance Act and Japan Housing Performance Indication Standards.

The Real Estate Companies Association of Japan represents large developers, home builders, real estate agents, banks and related companies (www.fdk.or.jp). The association publishes *Real Estate in Japan*, an annual handbook that provides an overview of the property market, including urban redevelopment and J-REITs, as well as trends, recent developments and statistics.

The Land Institute of Japan researches land use and prices, and real estate and urban planning issues (www.lij.jp). The institute's monthly statistical report includes sales volumes, the average price and size of condominiums and detached houses sold in Tokyo and Osaka, a diffusion index and bankruptcy information.

The Japan Real Estate Institute produces annual and biannual surveys of urban land prices, wooden house values, office and apartment rents, investor sentiment and expectations, agricultural land prices and farm rents, and timber lands (www.reinet.or.jp).

Miki Shoji produces a quarterly report of rents and vacancy rates for office space in Tokyo's Chiyoda, Chuo, Minato, Shibuya and Shinjuku wards (www.e-miki.com).

International

There is little English-language research on the Japanese residential property market. Japan is omitted from the global house price index produced by Knight Frank (www.knightfrank.co.uk). Other large real estate brokers, including CB Richard Ellis (www.cbre.com), Colliers Halifax (www.collliershalifax.com), Cushman & Wakefield (www.cushwake.com) and Jones Lang Lasalle (www.joneslanglasalle.com) cover Japan, but focus on office, retail and industrial space. Residential property is seldom mentioned.

Software
Architecture and design

Design software comes in three variations. First is the computer-aided design (CAD) software, like the products from Autodesk (http://autodesk.com). Intended for professionals, this software is powerful, expensive and has a steep learning curve, which may be hard to justify if you are only involved in one or two projects.

Second is consumer-oriented software from IMSI Design (www.imsidesign.com), SmartDraw (www.smartdraw.com), Punch! Software (www.punchsoftware.com) and others. Software in this category is less expensive—typically under $150—and less potent than professional products. It's also easier to learn.

Third, there is free software, like Google's Sketchup, a versatile, three-dimensional modeling package that can be used to design anything from a single room to a city (http://sketchup.google.com). Sketchup lets you import DWG files as well as colors and textures from JPG and PNG files. The basic version of Sketchup is a free download for computers using the Windows or Mac operating systems. Google sells a professional version of Sketchup and provides video tutorials on the Sketchup Website.

Floorplanner is a Web-based design tool that lets you create two- and three-dimensional room layouts and home designs (www.floorplanner.com). The basic program is free; a premium, paid service provides extra functionality. Swedish furniture retailer Ikea offers an online design tool that may be useful if you are planning to use that company's furniture (www.ikea.com).

Autodesk has a free, Web-based program called Project Dragonfly that allows you to create and furnish floor plans in two and three dimensions (http://dragonfly.autodesk.com). Autodesk also offers a free program called DWG Trueview that lets you view, print and annotate DWG files made with their professional CAD software. Similar programs are also available from Informative Graphics (www.infograph.com) and Autodwg (www.autodwg.com).

Paint and color

The Internet is a useful source of tools for generating color schemes for your new home. Paint manufacturers such as Dow Chemical operate sites with tools to help you choose a color theme (www.paintquality.com). Intended primarily for Web designers, Colorotate includes useful tools for understanding and working with color (www.colorotate.com).

Adobe's Kuler lets you build a color scheme from an image you upload to the site (http://kuler.adobe.com). Kuler uses the Adobe Swatch Exchange (ASE) format to send color information to Adobe's design products, such as Illustrator, InDesign and Photoshop. Kuler has a variety of other tools, including a color wheel, forums and searchable color themes. Colr.org (www.colr.org) and Colors Palette Generator (www.cssdrive.com/imagepalette/index.php) are similar to Kuler, but easier to use.

Colorjive lets you upload a photo of a room and virtually "paint" it (http://colorjive.com). A premium version, which allows you to store images online, is also available.

Blog myhomeideas has a calculator that allows you to enter the dimensions of a room and determine how much paint you'll need to buy (www.myhomeideas.com/project-calculator). The site uses imperial measurements and includes other calculators and guides.

Surveyors

Japan has two national organizations for surveyors: the Japan Association of Surveyors (www.jsurvey.jp) and the Japan Federation of Land and Building Surveyor's Association (www.chosashi.or.jp, Japanese only). The federation's Website contains contact information for regional associations, which have their own Websites.

Tax

International accounting firm Deloitte Touche Tohmatsu produces an English-language document called Japan: Individual Taxation (www.tohmatsu.com). The 2008/9 edition includes information on the tax treatment of rental income and capital gains from real estate, as well as tax credits for home loans and earthquake-proofing.

Ernst & Young provides information and advice on real estate taxation (www.ey.com).

The Japanese Institute of Certified Public Accountants' Website includes detailed, English-language information about the accounting profession in Japan, as well as corporate disclosure standards (www.hp.jicpa.or.jp). The Japanese portion of the Website has a "CPA search" function.

The Japan Federation of Certified Public Tax Accountants' Associations represents 15 regional tax accountants' associations (www.nichizeiren.or.jp). In addition to preparing documents, consulting and representing clients on tax matters, certified public tax accounts can offer property appraisal services. The Japanese portion of the association's Website includes detailed information about the tax system, as well as a "find a tax accountant" function.

International accounting firm KPMG publishes an annual guide called Taxation in Japan, which includes information on the taxation of individuals, companies and partnerships (www.kpmg.or.jp). International tax and real estate issues are also covered.

Termites

The Japan Termite Control Association maintains a Website with information about the services provided by its members (www.hakutaikyo.or.jp). The site's Japanese section includes photos of termites and the damage they cause, as well as contact information for regional termite control associations.

The University of California has detailed information about detecting, preventing and eliminating infestations of dry-wood termites (www.ipm.ucdavis.edu/PMG/PESTNOTES/pn7440.html).

Translation

The Japan Association of Translators is a trade group for professional translators and interpreters (http://members.jat.org). The association's Website includes a members list with profiles and contact details.

Google Translate lets you enter a word, a paragraph or an entire Website, which it then translates (www.translate.google.com). Japanese, English and other language pairs are supported. While the site is no substitute for a professional translator, it will give you a general idea of the original text's meaning. It's fast and free.

Transportation

Hyperdia is a database of routings and travel times between subway and train stations throughout Japan (www.hyperdia.com).

Typhoons

Tropical Storm Risk combines the efforts of the British Meteorological Office and several insurance and reinsurance companies to map and predict the progress of storms worldwide (www.tropicalstormrisk.com). The U.S.-based Cooperative Institute for Meteorological Satellite Studies offers a similar service (http://cimss.ssec.wisc.edu/tropic2/).

Universal design

The Center for Universal Design at North Carolina State University's College of Design has information for people who are building or renovating a home, including floor plans, checklists and design suggestions (www.ncsu.edu/ncsu/design/cud/).

A Practical Guide to Universal Home Design is available from the Iowa Program for Assistive Technology (www.uiowa.edu/infotech/universalhomedesign.htm).

Utilities

Gas

The Japan Gas Association has detailed English-language information about the city gas industry, including a listing of all of the gas suppliers in Japan and safety and environmental information (www.gas.or.jp).

Japan's two biggest gas companies, Tokyo Gas (www.tokyo-gas.co.jp) and Osaka Gas (www.osakagas.co.jp), have bilingual Websites with information for residential customers.

Electricity

The Japan Electric Power Information Center is the trade organization representing the nation's generating and distribution companies (www.jepic.or.jp). The center's Website includes links to all of Japan's electric companies as well as technical data.

Japan's two largest electrical companies, Tokyo Electric Power (www.tepco.co.jp) and Kansai Electric Power (www.kepco.co.jp), maintain English-language Websites.

NOTES

Demographic trends

1. *Statistical Handbook of Japan 2008*, (Statistics Bureau, Ministry of Internal Affairs and Communications, Government of Japan, 2008), 12, http://www.stat.go.jp/english/data/handbook/index.htm.

2. "White Paper on the Aging Society (Summary) FY 2007," (Cabinet Office, Government of Japan, 2008), 3, http://www8.cao.go.jp/kourei/english/annualreport/2007/2007.pdf.

3. "Japan's Affluent and HNWI Markets Consisted of 903,000 Households and Amounted to ¥254 Trillion in 2007, While Its Inheritance Market Will Expand to ¥102 Trillion by 2015," (Nomura Research Institute, 2008), http://www.nri.co.jp/english/news/2008/081001.html.

4. Tatsuya Ishikawa and Koichi Haji, "On the Financial Situation of Elderly Households: A Structural Analysis of Income, Expenditure, and Wealth," (NLI Research Institute, 2009), 4, http://www.nli-research.co.jp/english/economics/2009/eco090317.html.

5. Akio Doteuchi, "Family and Residence in the Gracefully Aging Society—Integrating Housing and Community," (NLI Research Institute, 2007), http://www.nli-research.co.jp/english/socioeconomics/2007/li070418.html.

6. *Population Statistics of Japan 2008*, (National Institute of Population and Social Security Research, Government of Japan, 2008), 4, http://www.ipss.go.jp/p-info/e/psj2008/PSJ2008.pdf.

7. F. Nishi and M. Kan, "Current Situation of Parasite-singles in Japan (Summary)," (Statistical Research and Training Institute, Ministry of Internal Affairs and Communications, Government of Japan, 2006), http://www.stat.go.jp/training/english/reseach/parasite_eng.pdf.

8. "Changes in Japan's Economic Society," (Ministry of Finance, Government of Japan, 2008), 4, http://www.mof.go.jp/english/tax/tax.htm.

9. H. Edison et al., "Japan: Selected Issues," (International Monetary Fund, 2004), 55, http://imf.org/external/pubs/ft/scr/2004/cr04247.pdf.

10. Robert Retherford and Naohiro Ogawa, "Japan's Baby Bust: Causes, Implications, and Policy Responses," (East-West Center, 2005), 14, http://www.eastwestcenter.org/fileadmin/stored/pdfs/POPwp118.pdf.

11. "Highlights of the Budget for FY2009," (Ministry of Finance, Government of Japan, 2008), 14, http://www.mof.go.jp/english/budget/budget.htm.

12. "Annual Health, Labour and Welfare Report 2007–2008: Part 1," (Ministry of Health, Labour and Welfare, Government of Japan, 2009), 23, http://www.mhlw.go.jp/english/wp/wp-hw2/index.html.

13. "Country Comparison: Total fertility rate," *CIA – The World Factbook*, (Central Intelligence Agency, United States Government, 2009), https://www.cia.gov/library/publications/the-world-factbook/rankorder/2127rank.html.

14. Arudou Debito, "What is a Japanese? Perspectives From a Naturalized Japanese Citizen," (2007), http://www.debito.org/tokaispeech062507.doc.

15. Jeffery Passel, "Growing Share of Immigrants Choose Naturalization," (The Pew Charitable Trusts, 2007), 3 & 26, http://www.pewtrusts.org/our_work_report_detail.aspx?id=20698.

16. "Revitalization of Japan and Strengthening its Competitiveness—Proposals for Creating a Japan as a Country Open to the World (executive summary)," (Japan Association of Corporate Executives, 2008), http://www.doyukai.or.jp/en/policyproposals/articles/pdf/080327a_english.pdf.

17. "27% of inns shun foreign guests," *The Asahi Shimbun* (English edition), October 11, 2008.

18. "Summary of the Results of Internal Migration in 2008," (Statistics Bureau, Ministry of Internal Affairs and Communications, Government of Japan, 2009), http://www.stat.go.jp/english/data/idou/2008np/index.htm.

19. Noboru Hashizume, "The Population Issue of Rural Regions in Japan," (Policy Research Institute, Ministry of Agriculture, Forestry and Fisheries, Government of Japan, 2005), http://www.fanea.org/symposium/the3rdFANEA.htm.

20. Kazuhiro Nishikawa, "Preventive Maintenance and National Land Management," (National Institute for Land and Infrastructure Management, Ministry of Land, Infrastructure, Transport and Tourism, Government of Japan, 2009), 2, http://www.nilim.go.jp/english/report/annual/annual2009/2.pdf.

The buying process

1. "Real Estate in Japan 2009," (The Real Estate Companies Association of Japan, 2009), 31, http://www.fdk.or.jp/en/pdf/rej2009.pdf.

2. Chihiro Shimizu et al, "Measuring the Cost of Imperfect Information in the Tokyo Housing Market," (University of Tokyo, 2003), 26, http://ideas.repec.org/p/tky/fseres/2003cf238.html.

3. Kiyohiko Nishimura and Chihiro Shimizu, "Distortion in Land Price Information: Mechanism in Sales Comparables and Appraisal Value Relation," (University of Tokyo, 2003), 1, http://www.e.u-tokyo.ac.jp/cirje/research/dp/2003/list.htm.

4. Hideaki Ozawa and Takuya Fujimoto, "The International Comparative Legal Guide to Real Estate 2009: Japan," (Global Legal Group, 2009), 209, http://www.iclg.co.uk/khadmin/Publications/pdf/2701.pdf.

5. Nishimura and Shimizu, "Distortion in Land Price Information: Mechanism in Sales Comparables and Appraisal Value Relation," 8.

6. Robert B. Cialdini, *Influence: The Psychology of Persuasion, Revised*, (Collins, 1998), 14.

7. Dan Ariely, *Predictably Irrational: The Hidden Forces That Shape Our Decisions*, (HarperCollins, 2009), 8.

8. *Statistical Handbook of Japan 2008*, (Statistics Bureau, Ministry of Internal Affairs and Communications, Government of Japan, 2008), 163, http://www.stat.go.jp/english/data/handbook/index.htm.

9. Tatsuya Ishikawa and Koichi Haji, "On the Financial Situation of Elderly Households: A Structural Analysis of Income, Expenditure, and Wealth," (NLI Research Institute, 2009), 4, http://www.nli-research.co.jp/english/economics/2009/eco090317.html.

10. Akio Doteuchi, "'Downsizing' of Housing and Lifestyles for a Low-Carbon Aging Society," (NLI Research Institute, 2008), http://www.nli-research.co.jp/english/socioeconomics/2008/li080626.pdf.

11. Akio Doteuchi, "Aging Issues in New Town Developments—The Tama New Town Case," (NLI Research Institute, 1998), http://crystal.nli-research.co.jp/english/socioeconomics/1998/li9805.html.

12. Kenji Utsumi and Hiroto Inoue, "Japan—Getting the Deal Through 2009," (Nagashima Ohno and Tsunematsu, 2009), 105, http://www.gettingthedealthrough.com.

13. Paul Previtera, "Tax Consequences of Cross-Border Investment in Japanese Real Estate," *Tax Notes International*, (2006), 152.

14. Takenaka Corporation, *Investing in Japan: An Introduction to Japanese Real Estate Business and Practices*, (Urban Land Institute, 2004), 84.

15. Naosuke Fujita and Hiroki Sugita, "Corporate Real Estate 2006/07: Japan," (O'Melveny & Myers LLP, 2006), 124.

16. A Quick Look at Housing in Japan, 2008 edition, (The Building Center of Japan, 2008), 36.

Choosing a location

1. Dan Ariely, Predictably Irrational: The Hidden Forces That Shape Our Decisions, (HarperCollins, 2009), 31.

2. "Growth strategy focuses on social infrastructure," The Japan Times, April 5, 2009, http://search.japantimes.co.jp/rss/nb20090405a1.html.

3. Chihiro Shimizu and Kiyohiko Nishimura, "Nonlinearity of Housing Price Structure: The Secondhand Condominium Market in the Tokyo Metropolitan Area," (University of Tokyo, 2007), 34, www.csis.u-tokyo.ac.jp/dp/86.pdf.

4. "Annual Health, Labour and Welfare Report 2007-2008: Part 1," (Ministry of Health, Labour and Welfare, Government of Japan, 2009), 23, http://www.mhlw.go.jp/english/wp/wp-hw2/index.html.

What to buy

1. A Quick Look at Housing in Japan, 6th edition, (The Building Center of Japan, 2008), 39.

2. Kei Sakamoto et al, "A Study on the Life Cycle Cost and Environmental Burden of a Long-Life House," (Presented at the 22nd Pan Pacific Congress of Real Estate Appraisers, Valuers and Counselors, Taipei, 2004), 30–31.

3. "Housing starts in Japan plunge 27.9% in 2009," (Japan Today, January 30, 2010), http://www.japantoday.com/category/business/view/housing-starts-in-japan-plunge-279-in-2009.

4. Hiroyuki Yoshida, "A Study of Earthquake Risk in Japan and its Peripheral Problems," (Presented at the 23rd Pan Pacific Congress of Real Estate Appraisers, Valuers and Counselors, San Francisco, 2006), 6.

5. "Center for Housing Renovation and Dispute Settlement Support," (2007), http://www.chord.or.jp/english/index.html.

6. "Environmental Report 2003," (Sekisui Chemical Co., Ltd., 2003), 34, http://www.sekisui.co.jp/csr/report/__icsFiles/afieldfile/2007/01/31/env_report_2003_e.pdf.

7. Yoshida, "A Study of Earthquake Risk in Japan and its Peripheral Problems," 8.

8. "Home Anti-seismic Test for Everyone," (The Japan Building Disaster Prevention Association, 2006), http://www.kenchiku-bosai.or.jp/english/index.html.

9. "Housing Inspections and Evaluations: Problems and How to Create Mechanisms to Solve Them," (Fujitsu Research Institute, 2005), http://jp.fujitsu.com/group/fri/en/column/message/200512/2005-12-01-1.html.

10. "Japan architect admits substandard work," The China Daily, December 15, 2005, http://www.chinadaily.com.cn/english/doc/2005-12/15/content_503607.htm.

11. "Elevator decree takes effect," The Japan Times, September 29, 2009, http://search.japantimes.co.jp/rss/nn20090929a4.html.

12. Chihiro Shimizu et al, "Nonlinearity of Housing Price Structure: The Secondhand Condominium Market in the Tokyo Metropolitan Area," (University of Tokyo, 2007), 31, http://www.csis.u-tokyo.ac.jp/dp/86.pdf.

13. Masahide Tanaka and Yoshinobu Kumata, "Problems of Decrepit Condominiums Furthering Aggravation of Urban Environment: Is Rebuilding Possible by Means of Reverse Mortgage System?," *Studies in Regional Science* 29, no. 2 (December 1999): 58, http://www.journalarchive.jst.go.jp/english/jnlabstract_en.php?cdjournal=srs1970&cdvol=29&noissue=2&startpage=58.

14. "Real Estate in Japan 2009," (The Real Estate Companies Association of Japan, 2009), 13, http://www.fdk.or.jp/en/publication.html.

15. Hideaki Ozawa and Takuya Fujimoto, "The International Comparative Legal Guide to Real Estate 2009: Japan," (Global Legal Group, 2009), 207, http://www.iclg.co.uk/khadmin/Publications/pdf/2701.pdf.

16. Takenaka Corporation, *Investing in Japan: An Introduction to Japanese Real Estate Business and Practices*, (Urban Land Institute, 2004), 84.

17. Shinichiro Iwata and Hisaki Yamaga, "Land Tenure Security and Home Maintenance: Evidence from Japan," (University of Tokyo, 2007), 14, http://www.e.u-tokyo.ac.jp/cirje/research/03research02dp.html.

18. "Introduction to the Building Standard Law," (The Building Center of Japan, 2009), 49.

Risk factors

1. "Administration of Cultural Affairs in Japan—Fiscal 2009," (Agency for Cultural Affairs, Government of Japan, 2009), 44, http://www.bunka.go.jp/english/pdf/chapter_06.pdf.

2. Charles Keally, "Japanese Archeology," (2003), http://www.t-net.ne.jp/~keally/jpnarch.html.

3. "Elimination of asbestos-related diseases," (World Health Organization, 2006), http://www.who.int/occupational_health/publications/asbestosrelateddisease/en/index.html.

4. "Asbestos," (American Cancer Society, 2006), http://www.cancer.org/docroot/PED/content/PED_1_3X_Asbestos.asp?sitearea=PED.

5. Laurie Kazan-Allen, "Asbestos: The Environmental Hazard," (AGH University of Science and Technology, 2006), 12, http://www.ceramika.agh.edu.pl/azbest06/2.pdf.

6. "History: 1960–1989," (W.R. Grace & Co., 2006), http://www.grace.com/About/History.aspx?timeframe=1960.

7. "Public Health Assessment, Libby Asbestos Site, Libby, Lincoln County, Montana," (Agency for Toxic Substances and Disease Registry, United States Government, 2003), http://www.atsdr.cdc.gov/HAC/pha/libby3/lby_p1.html.

8. "Highly toxic asbestos found in four buildings across Japan; current testing flawed," *The Mainichi Daily News*, November 12, 2009.

9. Kunihito Nishikawa et al, "Recent Mortality from Pleural Mesothelioma, Historical Patterns of Asbestos Use, and Adoption of Bans: A Global Assessment," *Environmental Health Perspectives* 116, no. 12 (December 2008): 1675–1680.

10. Jun Hongo, "Major asbestos suit kicks off in Tokyo," *The Japan Times*, July 24, 2008, http://search.japantimes.co.jp/cgi-bin/nn20080724a2.html.

11. "Case studies: ARI Technologies," (Japan External Trade Organization, 2008), http://www.jetro.org/content/595.

12. "Kubota CSR Report 2009," (Kubota Corp., 2009), 24, www.kubota.co.jp/eng/report/2009pdf/09_all.pdf.

13. "Chubu Electric Power ordered to compensate family over worker's asbestos-related death," *The Mainichi Daily News*, July 8, 2009.

14. "Medical Data Examination Results for Recognition of Designated Diseases under the Act on Asbestos Health Damage Relief," (Ministry of the Environment, Government of Japan, 2009), http://www.env.go.jp/en/headline/headline.php?serial=1056.

15. "Results of Monitoring Atmospheric Asbestos Concentrations in FY 2008," (Ministry of the Environment, Government of Japan, 2009), http://www.env.go.jp/en/headline/headline.php?serial=1038.

16. Kenji Morinaga et al, "Asbestos-Related Lung Cancer and Mesothelioma in Japan," *Industrial Health*, 39 (2001): 66.

17. Takumi Kishimoto et al, "Malignant Pleural Mesothelioma in Parts of Japan in Relationship to Asbestos Exposure," *Industrial Health* 42 (2004): 436.

18. Emily A. Su-lan Reber, "Buraku Mondai in Japan: Historical and Modern Perspectives and Directions for the Future," *Harvard Human Rights Journal* 12 (Spring 1999): 299.

19. Richard Werly, "The Burakumin, Japan's Invisible Outcasts," *Unesco Courier*, September 2001, http://findarticles.com/p/articles/mi_m1310/is_2001_Sept/ai_79007222/.

20. Tomiyoshi Ogawa et al, "The Aneha Scandal and Amendment of Japan's Building Standard Law," *Building Safety Journal*, (December 2007).

21. "Building agency cleared," *The Japan Times*, June 24, 2009, http://search.japantimes.co.jp/rss/nn20090624a5.html.

22. *A Quick Look at Housing in Japan, 2008 edition*, (The Building Center of Japan, 2008), 60.

23. "Current Activities of Earthquake Research Promotion in Japan," (Earthquake and Disaster-Reduction Research Division, Ministry of Education, Culture, Sports, Science and Technology, Government of Japan, 2006), 7, http://cais.gsi.go.jp/UJNR/6th/orally/O01_UJNR_Dobashi.pdf.

24. "Comprehensive evaluation of seismic activity," (The Headquarters for Earthquake Research Promotion, 2009), http://www.jishin.go.jp/main/index-e.html.

25. Harumi Yashiro et al, "How to Estimate the Economic Loss? Example from a Tokai Earthquake," (Asian Disaster Reduction Center, 2003), 7, http://www.proteccioncivil.org/es/DGPCE/Informacion_y_documentacion/catalogo/carpeta04/cd1987-2003/doc/b5/Economica/2aEstimEconomicF.Yoshimura.doc.

26. Etsuko Tsunozaki, "Disaster Reconstruction in Japan: Lessons Learned from the Kobe Earthquake," (Presented at the SAR Regional Conference on Hazard Risk Management, Mumbai, India, December 19, 2006), 11, http://www.worldbank.org/ieg/naturaldisasters/delhi/presentations/Session1/5-Japan_Kobe_Tsunozaki.pdf.

27. Hiroyuki Yoshida, "A Study of Earthquake Risk in Japan and its Peripheral Problems," (Presented at the 23rd Pan Pacific Congress of Real Estate Appraisers, Valuers and Counselors, San Francisco, 2006), 5.

28. Masayoshi Nakashima and Praween Chusilp, "A Partial View of Japanese Post-Kobe Seismic Design and Construction Practices," *Earthquake Engineering and Engineering Seismology* 4, no. 1 (September 2002): 11.

29. *A Quick Look at Housing in Japan, 2008 edition*, 39.

30. "Do you have a fire alarm installed in your home?," (Tokyo Fire Department, 2009), http://www.tfd.metro.tokyo.jp/eng/inf/firealarm.html.

31. "Urban Planning System in Japan," (Japan International Cooperation Agency; Ministry of Land, Infrastructure, Transport and Tourism, 2007), http://lvzopac.jica.go.jp.

32. Claer Barrett, "Britons face big losses on holiday homes," *The Financial Times*, August 28, 2009, http://www.ft.com/cms/s/0/a0774768-93f6-11de-9c57-00144feabdc0.html.

33. "Prefectures demand more tax revenues," The Japan Times, July 24, 2009, http://search.japantimes.co.jp/rss/nb20090724a1.html.

34. Maya Kaneko, "Bankrupt Yubari seeking funds as symbol of wrecked communities," The Japan Times, August 21, 2009, http://search.japantimes.co.jp/cgi-bin/nb20090821a1.html.

35. "Prefectures brace for revenue fall," The Japan Times, February 25, 2009, http://search.japantimes.co.jp/rss/nb20090225a9.html.

36. "Choshi hospital shuts its doors," The Daily Yomiuri, October 1, 2008.

37. "Financial Woes Spur 1st-Ever Closure Of Japanese Public Airport," (Nikkei.com, July 11, 2009), http://www.nni.nikkei.co.jp/e/fr/tnks/Nni20090710D10JFA10.htm.

38. Satoshi Simizutani and Noriko Inakura, "Japan's Public Long-term Care Insurance and the Financial Condition of Insurers: Evidence from Municipality-Level Data, Government Auditing Review," (The Board of Audit of Japan, Government of Japan, 2007), 29, http://www.jbaudit.go.jp/pr/pdf/e14d03.pdf.

39. "Nuclear Power in Japan," (World Nuclear Association, 2010), http://www.world-nuclear.org/info/inf79.html.

40. "(Summary) A Report on Safety Security of Kashiwazaki-Kariwa Nuclear Power Station after the Niigata-Chuetsu-Oki Earthquake," (Tokyo Electric Power Company, 2007), http://www.tepco.co.jp/en/press/corp-com/release/07072001-e.html.

41. "Criticality accident during periodic inspection," (World Nuclear News, April 23, 2007), http://www.world-nuclear-news.org/nerliste.aspx?id=11762.

42. "An Introduction to Indoor Air Quality," (Environmental Protection Agency, United States Government, 2009), http://www.epa.gov/iaq/voc.html.

43. Fumio Kondo et al, "Two Sensitive Sick-building Syndrome Patients Possibly Responding to p-Dichlorobenzene and 2-Ethyl-1-Hexanol: Case Report," Journal of Health Science 53, 1, (2007): 119.

44. "Indoor Air Facts No. 4 (revised) Sick Building Syndrome," (Environmental Protection Agency, United States Government, 2008), http://www.epa.gov/iaq/pubs/sbs.html.

45. "February 2005 Draft Report for Board," (Air Resources Board - California Environmental Protection Agency, 2005), 29, http://www.arb.ca.gov/research/indoor/ab1173/report0205/rpt0205-main.pdf.

46. Yoshika Sekine and Simon Watts, "Indoor Air Standards in Japan for Healthy Environment," (Presented at the 7th Indoor Air Quality 2006 Meeting, Braunschweig, November 15, 2006), 27–33, http://iaq.dk/iap/iaq2006/Sekine_IAQ2006.pdf.

47. Larry L. Needham and Ken Sexton, "Introduction and overview: Assessing children's exposure to hazardous environmental chemicals: an overview of selected research challenges and complexities," Journal of Exposure Analysis and Environmental Epidemiology 10, no. S6 (November 30, 2000): 611.

48. Karen Binkley, "Expert Opinion—Panic Attacks Induced by Olfactory Stimuli: An Emerging Paradigm for Idiopathic Environmental Intolerance (Multiple Chemical Sensitivity)," (Canadian Psychiatric Association, 2003), http://ww1.cpa-apc.org:8080/publications/archives/bulletin/2003/april/binkley.asp.

49. "Chemical sensitivity syndrome to make list of gov't-insured medical conditions," The Mainichi Daily News, June 12, 2009.

50. "Seller of apartment that caused sick house syndrome liable for damages," The Mainichi Daily News, October 2, 2009.

51. "Overview of Countermeasures Regarding Sick House Issues under the Amended Building Standard Law," (The Building Center of Japan, 2003), http://www.bcj.or.jp/en/services/evaluation/issue/issue02.html.

52. Greg Rogers, "Japan's brownfields brought to bear," *Environmental Finance*, (October 2007), http://www.environmental-finance.com/2007/0710oct/index.htm.

53. "Current status of the Brownfields Issue in Japan, Interim Report," (Expert Studying Group for Countermeasures against Brownfields, Ministry of the Environment, Government of Japan, 2007), 13, http://www.env.go.jp/en/water/soil/brownfields/interin-rep0703.pdf.

54. "Soil Contamination Countermeasures," (Soil Environment Management Division, Ministry of the Environment, Government of Japan, 2007), 5, http://www.env.go.jp/en/water/soil/contami_cm.pdf.

55. Fumikazu Yoshida, "High-tech Pollution in Asia," (Presented at the Ninth International Conference of Greening of Industry Network, Bangkok, January 21, 2001), 3–6, http://gin.confex.com/gin/archives/2001/papers/188.pdf.

56. "Environmental Quality Standards for Groundwater Pollution," (Ministry of the Environment, Government of Japan, 1999), http://www.env.go.jp/en/water/gw/gwp.html.

57. Kazuaki Nagata, "Tsukiji panel slammed during final meeting," *The Japan Times*, July 27, 2008, http://search.japantimes.co.jp/cgi-bin/nn20080727a3.html.

58. "PCB Waste Treatment Program," (Japan Environmental Safety Corporation, 2007), http://www.jesconet.co.jp/eg/pcb/pcb.html.

59. "Invitation of Proposals Concerning PCB Contaminated Solid Wastes Treatment Technologies," (Ministry of the Environment, Government of Japan, 2003), http://www.env.go.jp/en/recycle/ill_dum/pcb/index.html.

60. "Current status of the Brownfields Issue in Japan, Interim Report," 6.

61. Soil Contamination Countermeasures Act (Act No. 53 of 2002), Government of Japan, http://www.env.go.jp/en/laws/water/sccact.pdf.

62. "Highlights of the Budget for FY2009," (Ministry of Finance, Government of Japan, 2008), 24, http://www.mof.go.jp/english/budget/budget.htm.

63. "Budget guideline adopted," *The Japan Times*, July 3, 2009, http://search.japantimes.co.jp/rss/ed20090703a2.html.

64. "Tax revenues slide by record 13.2%," *The Japan Times*, July 3, 2009, http://search.japantimes.co.jp/rss/nb20090703a5.html.

65. "1st Half Corp Tax Revenue Falls Into Red, 1st Time Since FY60," (Nikkei.com, November 2, 2009), http://www.nni.nikkei.co.jp/e/fr/tnks/Nni20091102D02JF229.htm.

66. Yuliati Indrayani, "The invasive dry-wood termite Incisitermes minor (Hagen), in Japan: infestation, feeding ecology and control strategies," *Sustainable humanosphere: Bulletin of Research Institute for Sustainable Humanosphere*, Kyoto University, 3, (August 2007): 34–35.

67. Teruko Sato, "Fundamental Characteristics of Flood Risk in Japan's Urban Areas," (2006), 31, http://www.terrapub.co.jp/e-library/nied/pdf/023.pdf.

68. "Typhoon Isewan (Vera) and Its Lessons," (Japan Water Forum, 2005), 7, http://www.waterforum.jp/jpn/katrina/Typhoon_Isewan.pdf.

69. "Data," (Arakawa-Joryu River Management Office, Ministry of Land, Infrastructure, Transport and Tourism, Government of Japan, 2006).

70. "Arakawa River flood could submerge 97 subway stations in Tokyo, study shows," *The Mainichi Daily News*, January 24, 2009.

71. "3,500 Tokyo fatalities if Arakawa overflows," *The Daily Yomiuri*, September 10, 2008.

72. "Landslides," (United Nations University, 2008), 2, http://www.unu.edu/media/archives/2006/files/mre01-06.pdf.

73. "Toponymic Guidelines for Map Editors and other Editors (Third Edition, 2007)" (Geographical Survey Institute, Government of Japan, 2007), http://www.gsi.go.jp/ENGLISH/page_e30065.html#3-1.

74. "Crimes in Japan 2007," (National Police Agency, Government of Japan, 2008), 24, http://www.npa.go.jp/english/seisaku5/20081008.pdf.

75. "Yakuza and real estate," *The Asahi Shimbun* (English edition), March 11, 2008.

76. Peter Hill, "Heisei Yakuza: Burst Bubble and *Botaiho*," (University of Oxford, 2002), 11, http://ssjj.oxfordjournals.org/cgi/reprint/6/1/1.

77. Jake Adelstein, *Tokyo Vice: An American Reporter on the Police Beat in Japan*, 1st ed. (Pantheon, 2009)

78. "Urban Planning System in Japan," 66.

Mortgages

1. Susan Woodward, "A Study of Closing Costs for FHA Mortgages," (Urban Institute, 2008), http://www.urban.org/publications/411682.html.

2. Nobuyoshi Yamori and Kazumine Kondo, "How has Japan Housing Finance Agency's Flat 35 affected regional housing loan markets?," *Government Auditing Review* 15, (March 2008), 65, http://www.jbaudit.go.jp/pr/pdf/e15d04.pdf.

3. Birgit Baxendale, "Japanese City Banks: Unwarranted Housing Loan Expectations," (Federal Reserve Bank of San Francisco, 2005), 2, http://www.frbsf.org/publications/banking/asiafocus/2005/AsiaFocus-Sep05.pdf.

4. Michael Turner et al, "On the Impact of Credit Payment Reporting on the Financial Sector and Overall Economic Performance in Japan," (Information Policy Institute, 2007), 14, http://perc.net/files/downloads/Japan.pdf.

5. The rights of non-citizens: final report of the Special Rapporteur, David Weissbrodt," UN Sub-Commission on the Promotion and Protection of Human Rights, 2003), 13, http://www.unhcr.org/refworld/category,REFERENCE, UNSUBCOM,,,3f46114c4,0.html.

Insurance

1. "Annual Report 2008," (Japan Earthquake Reinsurance Co., 2008), 12, http://www.nihonjishin.co.jp/disclosure/index.html.

Tax

1. Takenaka Corporation, *Investing in Japan: An Introduction to Japanese Real Estate Business and Practices*, (Urban Land Institute, 2004), 33–36.

2. "Japan: Individual Taxation, 2008/09 Edition," (Deloitte Touche Tohmatsu, 2009), 7, http://www.deloitte.com/dtt/cda/doc/content/JP_individualtaxation_2009.pdf.

3. Paul Previtera, "Tax Consequences of Cross-Border Investment in Japanese Real Estate," *Tax Notes International*, (2006), 153.

4. "2008 Income Tax Guide for Foreigners," (National Tax Agency, Government of Japan, 2008), 65, http://www.nta.go.jp/foreign_language/index.htm.

5. "Guide to Metropolitan Taxes for 2008," (Tokyo Metropolitan Government, 2008), 68, http://www.tax.metro.tokyo.jp/book/guidebookgaigo/guidebook2008e.pdf.

6. "Comprehensive Handbook of Japanese Taxes 2006," (Ministry of Finance, Government of Japan, 2006), 148, http://www.mof.go.jp/english/tax/taxes2006e.htm.

7. "Taxation in Japan 2008," (KPMG Japan, 2008), 101, http://www.kpmg.or.jp/english/resources/index.html.

8. Kenji Ustumi and Hiroto Inoue, "Japan - Getting the Deal Through 2009," (Nagashima Ohno and Tsunematsu, 2009), 106, http://www.gettingthedealthrough.com.

A custom-designed home

1. "Landmark Study Finds Increased Productivity, Lower Vacancy and Higher Rents in Green Buildings," (CB Richard Ellis, 2009), http://www.cbre.com/EN/AboutUs/MediaCentre/2009/Pages/110209.aspx.

2. "Life-cycle assessment proves how environmentally friendly LED lamps are," (OSRAM GmbH, 2009), http://www.osram-os.com/osram_os/EN/Press/Press_Releases/Company_Information/LED-life-cycle-assessment.jsp.

3. Philip Jodidio, *Architecture in Japan*, (Taschen, 2006), 8.

4. Dana Buntrock, *Japanese Architecture as a Collaborative Process: Opportunities in a Flexible Construction Culture*, illustrated edition, (Taylor & Francis, 2002), 149.

5. "Urban Planning System in Japan," (Japan International Cooperation Agency; Ministry of Land, Infrastructure, Transport and Tourism, 2007), 16, http://lvzopac.jica.go.jp.

6. Takenaka Corporation, *Investing in Japan: An Introduction to Japanese Real Estate Business and Practices*, (Urban Land Institute, 2004), 53.

7. Yoshitsugu Kanemoto, "Housing Question in Japan," (University of Tokyo, 1997), 41, http://www.e.u-tokyo.ac.jp/~kanemoto/jhouse5.pdf.

8. Jun Endo, "Jichinsai," (Encyclopedia of Shinto, 2007), http://eos.kokugakuin.ac.jp/modules/xwords/entry.php?entryID=1043.

Investment property

1. "Dwellings by Tenure, Ratio of Owned Houses by Prefecture (1983–2008)," (Statistics Bureau, Ministry of Internal Affairs and Communications, Government of Japan, 2008), http://www.stat.go.jp/english/data/nenkan/1431-18.htm.

2. "Dwellings Used Exclusively for Living and Area of Floor Space per Dwelling by Tenure and Type of Building (1993–2008)," (Statistics Bureau, Ministry of Internal Affairs and Communications, Government of Japan, 2008), http://www.stat.go.jp/english/data/nenkan/1431-18.htm.

3. Tatsuya Ishikawa, "The Current Situation of Japan's Housing Market, and Policy Implications of the Projected Population Decrease," (NLI Research Institute, 2003), 10, http://www.nli-research.co.jp/english/economics/2003/eco030203.pdf.

4. Shinichi Tokuda, "Net a new tool for apartment hunters," *The Japan Times*, February 27, 2010, http://search.japantimes.co.jp/cgi-bin/nn20100227f1.html.

5. "Useful tips to find housing in Japan," (University of Tokyo, 2008), 11, http://dir.u-tokyo.ac.jp/files/Housing20080418_e.pdf.

6. "Tenant caused 'mental anguish' by rent collectors awarded 50,000 yen," *The Mainichi Daily News*, February 19, 2009.

7. "Trusted Rental Housing Project," (Promotion Council for Anshin-Chintai Housing), 44, http://www.mlit.go.jp/jutakukentiku/house/torikumi/anshin/minkanguide/minkanguide3e.pdf.

8. Miki Seko and Kazuto Sumita, "Fixed Term Contracts versus Open-ended Contracts in the Japanese Rental Housing Market," (Presented at the 13th Asian Real Estate Society Annual Meeting and International Conference, Shanghai, July 12–15, 2008), 3, http://asres2008.shufe.edu.cn/session/papers/h32.pdf.

9. Miki Tanikawa, "Lease changes change Japan," International Herald Tribune, November 21, 2006, http://www.nytimes.com/2006/11/21/realestate/21iht-release.3611728.html?_r=1.

10. Masayuki Nakagawa et al, "Earthquake risk and housing rents: Evidence from the Tokyo Metropolitan Area," Regional Science and Urban Economics 37 (1), 87–99 (January 2007): 98, www.econ.hit-u.ac.jp/~makoto/PDF/RSUE_2007_37.pdf.

11. "Trusted Rental Housing Project," 44–46.

12. Seko and Sumita, "Fixed Term Contracts versus Open-ended Contracts in the Japanese Rental Housing Market," 2.

13. "Trusted Renting Support Business: Apartment Search Guidebook," (Promotion Council for Anshin-Chintai Housing), 34, http://www.mlit.go.jp/jutakukentiku/house/torikumi/anshin/heyasagashi2.pdf.

14. Minoru Matsutani, "Shakeup in tenant terms," The Japan Times, August 1, 2009, http://search.japantimes.co.jp/cgi-bin/nn20090801f1.html.

15. Ryuji Nakagawa, "Tenant renewal fees ruled illegal," The Asahi Shimbun (English edition), July 29, 2009.

16. Philip Brasor, "Media plays down landmark rent ruling," The Japan Times, September 6, 2009, http://search.japantimes.co.jp/cgi-bin/fd20090906pb.html.

17. "Trusted Renting Support Business: Apartment Search Guidebook," 46.

18. "The blacklist is back," (Cat Foreheads & Rabbit Hutches, October 1, 2009), http://catforehead.wordpress.com/2009/10/01/the-blacklist-is-back/.

19. "Landlord poll finds a quarter turn elderly away," The Japan Times, May 10, 2000, http://search.japantimes.co.jp/cgi-bin/nn20000510b4.html.

20. A Quick Look at Housing in Japan, 6th edition, (The Building Center of Japan, 2008), 42.

21. Jun-ichi Goda, "Housing Policies for an Aged Society in Japan," (Presented at the Baby Boomers Aging in the World: Challenges and Policies, Nagoya, Japan, April 5, 2007), 26, http://us-foundation.org/pdfs/ppt_gouda_0407.pdf.

22. "Disposable Homes," (The Economist Intelligence Unit, 2009), 8.

23. Hidetaka Yoneyama, "Potential for Reviving Dilapidated Condominiums Utilizing Funds," (Fujitsu Research Institute, July 1, 2008), http://jp.fujitsu.com/group/fri/en/column/economic-topics/2008/2008-07-01-1.html.

24. "Comparative payoffs," (Yen for Living, October 22, 2009), http://blog.japantimes.co.jp/yen-for-living/comparative-payoffs/.

25. Chihiro Shimizu et al, "Nonlinearity of Housing Price Structure: The Secondhand Condominium Market in the Tokyo Metropolitan Area," (University of Tokyo, 2007), 29, 32, www.csis.u-tokyo.ac.jp/dp/86.pdf.

26. Naosuke Fujita and Hiroki Sugita, "Corporate Real Estate 2006/07: Japan," (O'Melveny & Myers LLP, 2006), 127.

27. Paul Previtera, "Tax Consequences of Cross-Border Investment in Japanese Real Estate," *Tax Notes International*, (2006), 152.

Niseko

1. "Report on the Current Situation of Foreign Tourist Visits and Investment in Niseko Area (Summary)," (JETRO Hokkaido, 2006), 2, http://www.jetro.go.jp/jfile/report/05001141/05001141_001_BUP_10.pdf.

2. "About Niseko," (Niseko Promotion Board, 2009), http://www.nisekotourism.com/en/about-niseko.

3. Kanako Takahara, "Boom time for Hokkaido ski resort area," *The Japan Times*, July 8, 2008, http://search.japantimes.co.jp/cgi-bin/nb20080708a1.html.

4. "Japan Tourism Agency," (Japan Tourism Agency, Ministry of Land, Infrastructure,Transport and Tourism, Government of Japan, 2008), http://www.mlit.go.jp/kankocho/en/.

5. "Hokkaido Toya Charter Helicopter," (Hokkaido Aviation Co., 2009), http://www.hokkaido-koku.co.jp/vip3.htm.

6. "Chitose-Niseko copter flights start," *The Japan Times*, March 4, 2009, http://search.japantimes.co.jp/rss/nb20090304a6.html.

7. "Hokkaido Shinkansen Bullet Train Line," (Hokkaido Bureau, Ministry of Land, Infrastructure, Transport and Tourism, Government of Japan, 2009), http://www.mlit.go.jp/hkb/train_e.html.

8. "International ATM now available in Hirafu Village!," (Niseko Promotion Board, 2009), http://www.nisekotourism.com/event-news/detail.php?lang=en&id=247.

9. "Report on the Current Situation of Foreign Tourist Visits and Investment in Niseko Area (Summary)," 5.

10. Michiyo Nakamoto, "Ill wind for developers as Zephyr folds," *The Financial Times*, July 22, 2008, http://www.ft.com/cms/s/0/9d8f9694-5785-11dd-916c-000077b07658.html.

Other opportunities

1. "Real Estate in Japan 2009," (The Real Estate Companies Association of Japan, 2009), 54, http://www.fdk.or.jp/en/publication.html.

2. "Tokyo Office Vacancies Rise To 8.25% In Jan," (Nikkei.com, February 4, 2010), http://www.nni.nikkei.co.jp/e/fr/tnks/Nni20100204D04SS492.htm.

3. "Basic indicators on food, agriculture and rural areas," (Ministry of Agriculture, Forestry and Fisheries, Government of Japan, 2007), 61, http://www.maff.go.jp/e/annual_report/2007/pdf/e_indi.pdf.

4. Roger Martini and Shingo Kimura, "Evaluation of Agricultural Policy Reforms in Japan," (Organisation for Economic Co-operation and Development, 2009), 10, http://www.oecd.org/dataoecd/26/45/42791674.pdf.

5. "Basic indicators on food, agriculture and rural areas," 60.

6. "Fact Sheet No. 1: Why Agriculture Needs Different Treatment in Trade Rules?," (Ministry of Agriculture, Forestry and Fisheries, Government of Japan, 2003), 2, www.maff.go.jp/e/pdf/factsheet.pdf.

7. "80 day care firms receive warnings," *The Japan Times*, May 29, 2009, http://search.japantimes.co.jp/rss/nn20090529b2.html.

8. "Waiting list for nursing homes put at 400,000," *The Japan Times*, January 27, 2009, http://search.japantimes.co.jp/rss/nn20090127a7.html.

9. "Aims of Establishing Long-term Care Insurance," (Ministry of Health, Labour and Welfare, Government of Japan, 2002), http://www.mhlw.go.jp/english/topics/elderly/care/1.html.

10. Shinya Matsuda and Mieko Yamamoto, "Long-term care insurance and integrated care for the aged in Japan," *International Journal of Integrated Care* 1 (September 2001), http://www.ncbi.nlm.nih.gov/pmc/articles/PMC1484411/.

11. Setsuko Kamiya, "Comsn president to step down over certification fraud," *The Japan Times*, June 9, 2007, http://search.japantimes.co.jp/cgi-bin/nn20070609a1.html.

12. "Negligence probed in fire at senior home," *The Japan Times*, March 24, 2009, http://search.japantimes.co.jp/cgi-bin/nn20090324a4.html.

13. Chris Cooper and Makiko Kitamura, "DiCaprio Statue, $30 Rooms Boost Japan's Love Hotels," (Bloomberg, May 21, 2009), http://www.bloomberg.com/apps/news?pid=newsarchive&sid=aDRpAsdCJ7dw.

14. Tim Kelly, "Love for Sale," (Forbes.com, June 5, 2006), http://www.forbes.com/forbes/2006/0605/106.html.

15. Kanako Takahara, "No-tell love hotels cash in catering to the carnal," *The Japan Times*, October 16, 2007, http://search.japantimes.co.jp/cgi-bin/nn20071016i1.html.

16. Mayumi Saito, "Half a room, without a view," *The Japan Times*, September 8, 2009, http://search.japantimes.co.jp/cgi-bin/fl20090908zg.html.

17. Mariko Sanchanta, "Sayonara to the Rabbit Hutch: Living With Roommates in Japan," *The Wall Street Journal*, December 30, 2009, http://online.wsj.com/article/SB126213678598709767.html?mod=WSJ_hpp_MIDDLENexttoWhatsNewsSecond.

Useful information

1. Kazuaki Nagata, "DVD offers foreigners ins, outs of rental market," *The Japan Times*, August 1, 2009, http://search.japantimes.co.jp/cgi-bin/nn20090801a5.html.

LIST OF FIGURES

Charts

Tables
Page 52. Sample condominium purchase in downtown Tokyo
Source: www.fudousan.or.jp and www.eloan.co.jp.

Page 53. Sample condominium purchase in Tokyo's western suburbs
Source: www.fudousan.or.jp and www.eloan.co.jp.

Page 120. Stamp tax rates
Source: *Comprehensive Handbook of Japanese Taxes 2006*, Ministry of Finance.

Page 135. Urban zoning
Source: *Urban Planning System in Japan*, Japan International Cooperation Agency and the Ministry of Land, Infrastructure, Transport and Tourism.

Page 150. Sample purchase and rental income figures
Source: Akasaka Real Estate.

Page 192. International brands available in Japan

PHOTO CREDITS

All of the photography in this book was shot by the author, with the following exceptions. The cover photo and photo on page 66 are courtesy of Misawa Homes Co, Ltd. The image on page 162 is courtesy of Hokkaido Tracks. The author's photo is by Graham Uden (www.udenphoto.com).

INDEX

ABOUT THE AUTHOR

Christopher Dillon is an award-winning writer and entrepreneur based in Hong Kong.

In 2002, he bought and renovated a floor in an office building in Hong Kong's Central business district. Since then, he has purchased and refurbished a luxury apartment on the west side of Hong Kong Island and transformed a derelict steam laundry into a multimedia studio. That experience inspired his first book, *Landed: The expatriate's guide to buying and renovating property in Hong Kong*, and a companion audiobook.

Christopher lived in Tokyo from 1989 to 1992. He travels to Japan regularly with his consulting business, Dillon Communications Ltd.

www.ingramcontent.com/pod-product-compliance
Lightning Source LLC
Chambersburg PA
CBHW061200220326
41599CB00025B/4543